108 GAUDIYA VAISHNAVA BOOKS

DROPS OF DEVOTION

HARI GOPINATH DAS

A. C. Bhaktivedanta Swami Prabhupada Founder Acharya ISKCON

"All the devotees connected with the Krishna consciousness movement must read all the books that have been translated (the Caitanya-caritamrta, Srimad-Bhagavatam, Bhagavad-Gita and others); otherwise, after some time, they will simply eat, sleep and fall down from their position. Thus they will miss the opportunity to attain an eternal, blissful life of transcendental pleasure." - Srila Prabhupada's purport, Madhya 25.279

Contents

Mangalacarana

Sri Guru Pranama
Om ajnana-timirandhasya jnananjana-salakaya
cakshur unmilitam yena tasmai sri-gurave namah
When will Srila Rupa Gosvami Prabhupada, who has
established within this material world the mission to fulfill
the desire of Lord Caitanya, give me shelter under his lotus
feet?

Mangalacarana
Vande 'ham sri-guroh sri-yuta-pada-kamalam
sri-gurun vaishnavams ca
sri-rupam sagrajatam saha-gana-raghunathanvitam tam sa
jivam
sadvaitam savadhutam parijana-sahitam
krishna-caitanya-devam
sri-radha-krishna-padan saha-gana-lalita-
sri-visakhanvitams ca
I offer my respectful obeisances unto the lotus feet of my
spiritual master and of all the other preceptors on the path
of devotional service. I offer my respectful obeisances
unto all the Vaishnavas and unto the six Gosvamis,
including Srila Rupa Gosvami, Srila Sanatana Gosvami,
Raghunatha dasa Gosvami, Jiva Gosvami, and their
associates. I offer my respectful obeisances unto Advaita
Acarya Prabhu, Sri Nityananda Prabhu, Sri Caitanya
Mahaprabhu, and all His devotees, headed by Srivasa
Thakura. I then offer my respectful obeisances unto the
lotus feet of Lord Krishna, Srimati Radharani, and all the
gopis, headed by Lalita and Visakha.

Srila Prabhupada Pranati

Nama om vishnu-padaya krishna-preshthaya bhu-tale
srimate bhaktivedanta-svamin iti namine
I offer my respectful obeisances unto His Divine Grace A.
C. Bhaktivedanta Swami Prabhupada, who is very dear to
Lord Krishna, having taken shelter at His lotus feet.
namas te sarasvate deve gaura-vani-pracarine
nirvisesha-sunyavadi-pascatya-desa-tarine
Our respectful obeisances are unto you, O spiritukindly
preaching the message of Lord Caitanyadeva and
delivering the Western countries, which are filled with
impersonalism and voidism.

Panca-tattva Maha-mantra

(jaya) sri-Krishna-Caitanya Prabhu Nityananda
sri-advaita gadadhara srivasadi-gaura-bhakta-vrinda
Maha Mantra
HARE KRISHNA HARE KRISHNA
KRISHNA KRISHNA HARE HARE
HARE RAMA HARE RAMA
RAMA RAMA HARE HARE

Other Publications by Hari Gopinath Das :

- **The Manual of Life - Gita : Tips and Tricks to Understand Srimad Bhagavad Gita**
- **Gita for Gen Z: Gita for Teenagers**

For further information and important shlokas of books mentioned in this compendium, visit Harigopinath Das website https://harigopinathdas.com/

Preface

The Gaudiya Vaishnava tradition, a spiritual path from India, has a rich history built on its many sacred books. These aren't just books; they're guides for living a life of devotion and expressions of deep love for the divine.

What Awaits Within This Collection

- Mystical **prayers** that resonate beyond time
- **Philosophical** treatises that challenge and expand your understanding
- Devotional **biographies** that invite you to walk alongside saints
- **Practical instructions** that illuminate how to live as a devotee

This book is offered as a **humble bridge,** a concise yet comprehensive guide to the essence of these 108 jewels of Gaudiya Vaishnavism. Within these pages, you will find a summary of each text, offering a glimpse into its key themes, its unique contribution to the philosophical tapestry, and the specific aspects of devotional life it illuminates. **The aim is not to replace the original works, but rather to provide a foundational familiarity** – to introduce you to the names, the philosophical progression, and the specific focus of each book.

May this humble endeavor serve as a stepping stone, encouraging a deeper engagement with the original sources when the opportunity arises. **Be empowered to choose which book resonates most with your current needs and interests.** When time allows, you will have a clearer direction on where to delve deeper, guided by an initial understanding of each work. May it foster a greater appreciation for the profound wisdom of our acharyas and inspire a more enriched and focused journey on the path of bhakti.

May every book in this collection be **a drop of devotion** that awakens your soul.

For further information and important shlokas of books mentioned in this compendium, visit Harigopinath Das website https://harigopinathdas.com/

Acknowledgements

At the culmination of this endeavor, my heart swells with gratitude for the countless sources of inspiration and support that have made this book a reality. First and foremost, I offer my deepest obeisances and heartfelt thanks to my beloved Guru Maharaj, **His Holiness Radhanath Swami.** His unwavering guidance, boundless compassion, and profound teachings have been the very foundation upon which this work has been built. His example of selfless service and dedication to the principles of Gaudiya Vaishnavism has been a constant source of light and motivation.

It is with profound humility and gratitude that I bow at the lotus feet of the esteemed **previous acharyas** and authors whose works form the foundation of this compendium. Their writings are a treasure, illuminating the path of bhakti, and it is my sincere hope that this summary will serve as an invitation, encouraging readers to delve into the original works and thereby deepen their understanding and enrich their spiritual lives. May this effort please them.

I also wish to express my eternal gratitude to **my father**, the late Shri Ramesh Acharya. Though physically absent, his early spiritual influence and the values he instilled continue to resonate deeply within me. His blessings, I believe, have paved the way for this humble offering.

To my **dear mother**, Astasakhi Devi Dasi, your unwavering faith, love, and encouragement have been a constant source of strength. Your dedication to the path of devotion has been a guiding beacon throughout my life.

My heartfelt appreciation extends to my **beloved wife**, Ratnamayi Devaki Devi Dasi, for her unwavering support, patience, and understanding throughout the writing process. Her partnership in spiritual life has been invaluable.

To my **dear son**, Achintya Acharya, you are a constant source of joy and inspiration. Witnessing your innocent faith strengthens my own resolve on this path.

A special note of gratitude is due to the **ISKCON Desire Tree website**. This invaluable resource has generously provided access to a vast collection of authentic Gaudiya Vaishnava literature, making these profound teachings freely available and greatly facilitating the research and understanding necessary for this book.

I am also deeply indebted to the cherished **devotee community** of our Saturday Bhagavatam class. Our collective study, discussions, and shared love for the teachings have enriched my understanding immeasurably and provided a supportive environment for this project to take shape.

Finally, I extend my sincere thanks to the wider devotee community of ISKCON whose guidance, encouragement, and inspiring examples have been a constant source of strength and illumination on this journey of understanding and sharing the profound wisdom of Gaudiya Vaishnavism.

Any merit found within these pages is solely due to the blessings of these spiritual guides and well-wishers. <u>Any imperfections are humbly offered as my own.</u>

108 Names Alphabetically

1. Ananda Vrindavana Campu PS 5
2. Bābājī Mahārāja: Two Beyond Duality PE 13
3. Bhagavad Gita as It Is PF 3
4. Bhagavad Gita as it is Further explained PH 5
5. Bhajana Rahasya PH 23
6. Bhakti Ratnakar PE 8
7. Bhakti-rasāyanam PH 11
8. Bhavana Sara Sangraha PES 11
9. Bhavartha-dipika PH 7
10. Books by Srila Prabhupada & his disciples PF 10
11. Brahmana and Vaishnava PH 27
12. Brihad Bhagavatamrita PH 14
13. Brihad Vaishnava Toshani PES 7
14. Caitanya Bhāgavata PE 2
15. Camatkar Candrika PS 9
16. Chaitanya Charitamrita PF 9
17. Chaitanya Charitamrita PE 1
18. Chaitanya Mangala PE 6
19. Chaitanya Shikshamrita PH 22

20. Commentaries Chaitanya Charitamrita SB PE 5
21. Dana Keli Kaumudi PS 4
22. Dig-darshini Tika PH 29
23. Foundational- Vedas/Upanishad/Itihas PF 1
24. Gaura Ganoddesha Dipika PE 7
25. Gita-mala (A Garland of Songs) P 4
26. Gitavali (Song collection) P 5
27. Gopala Campu PS 1
28. Govinda Bhashya PH 6
29. Govinda Lilamrita PES 3
30. Govinda Vrindavanastakam PL 1
31. Hamsaduta PES 9
32. Hari Bhakti Vilasa PH 15
33. Harinama Chintamani PHH 1
34. Jagannatha Mandir PL 9
35. Jaiva Dharma PH 21
36. Kalyana Kalpataru P 6
37. Krishna-bhavanamrita PES 8
38. Krsna lila stave PS 10
39. Krsna Samhita PS 8
40. Krsna, the Supreme Personality of Godhead PS 12
41. Laghu-bhagavatamrita PH 16
42. Laghu-toṣaṇī PH 9
43. Lalita Madhava PS 3
44. Madhurya Kadambini PES 4
45. Mathura Mahatmya PL 3
46. Mathura mandala Parikrama PL 4
47. Mukunda Mala Stotra PF 7
48. Namacarya: The Life of Srila Haridasa Thakura PE 9
49. Narottama Vilasa PE 11
50. Navadvipa-sataka PL 7
51. Padyavali P 9
52. Prakrita Rasa Shata Dushani PES 6

85. Sri Sri Navadvipa Bhava Taranga PL 8
86. Sri Sri Radha Krsna Ganoddesa dipika PH30
87. Śrī Vedānta-syāmantaka PH 19
88. Śrī Vilāpa Kusumāñjali PES 2
89. Sri Vrindavana Mahimanrta PL 5
90. Srila Bhaktivinoda Thakura: His Life and Works PE 12
91. Srila Prabhupada-lilamrta PE 15
92. Srimad Bhagavata Arka Marichimala PH 12
93. Srimad Bhagavatam PF 8
94. Stava-mala P 7
95. Stavamrita Lahiri P 10
96. Stavavali P 8
97. Sutra upasana Vaisnava puja vidhi PH 33
98. Tattva Sutra PH 24
99. Tattva Viveka (Discerning the Truth) PH 26
100. The Nectar of Instruction PF 4
101. Uddhava Sandesha PES 10
102. Ujjvala Nilamani PES 1
103. Ujjvala Nilamani Kiranah PES 16
104. Upakhyane Upadesa PS 11
105. Vaishnava Siddhanta Mala PH 13
106. Vaisnava Etiquette PH 31
107. Vidagdha Madhava PS 2
108. Vraja-riti-chintamani PL 2

<u>CODES</u>

Primary foundation **PF** Philosophy **PH** Philosophy Holy Name **PHH** Personality **PE** Prayers **P** Places **PL** Pastime **PS** Personal Esoteric **PES**

CHAPTER TWO

108 Books in 7 P's

PRIMARY FOUNDATION (PF)

1. Foundational- Vedas/Upanishad/Itihas
2. Sikshashtakam
3. Bhagavad Gita As It Is
4. The Nectar of Instruction
5. Sri Bhakti Rasamrita Sindhu /Nectar of Devotion
6. Sri Isopanisad
7. Mukunda Mala Stotra
8. Srimad Bhagavatam
9. Chaitanya Charitamrita
10. Books by Srila Prabhupada & his disciples

PHILOSOPHY (PH)

1. Sri Caitanyopanishad
2. Sarartha Varshini Tika on Bhagavad Gita
3. Śrī Gita-bhūṣaṇa
4. Rasika ranjana and Vidvat Ranjan

5. Bhagavad Gita as it is Further explained in lectures book
6. Govinda Bhashya
7. Bhavartha-dipika
8. Sri Brhad-vaisnava-tosani
9. Laghu-toṣaṇī
10. Sarartha Darshini
11. Bhakti-rasāyanam
12. Srimad Bhagavata Arka Marichimala
13. Vaishnava Siddhanta Mala
14. Brihad Bhagavatamrita
15. Hari Bhakti Vilasa
16. Laghu-bhagavatamrita
17. Sat Sandarbhas (Six Treatises)
18. Śrī Aiśvarya-Kādambinī
19. Śrī Vedānta-syāmantaka
20. Prameya Ratnavali
21. Jaiva Dharma
22. Chaitanya Shikshamrita
23. Bhajana Rahasya
24. Tattva Sutra
25. Śrī Daśa Mūla Tattva
26. Tattva Viveka (Discerning the Truth)
27. Brahmana and Vaishnava
28. Sarva-samvadini
29. Dig-darshini Tika
30. Sri Sri Radha Krsna Ganoddesa dipika
31. Vaisnava Etiquette
32. Sat Kriya Sara Dipika
33. Sutra upasana Vaisnava puja vidhi

<u>HOLYNAME (PHH)</u>

1. Harinama Chintamani
2. Śrī Godruma Kalpāṭavī

PERSONALITIES (PE)

1. Chaitanya Charitamrita
2. Caitanya Bhāgavata
3. Śrī Kṛṣṇa Caitanya Caritra Mahākāvyam
4. Śrī Caitanya Mahāprabhu: His Life and Precepts
5. Commentaries on Chaitanya Charitamrita & Bhagavatam
6. Chaitanya Mangala
7. Gaura Ganoddesha Dipika
8. Bhakti Ratnakar
9. Namacarya: The Life of Srila Haridasa Thakura
10. Sri Nityananda Caritamrta
11. Narottama Vilasa
12. Srila Bhaktivinoda Thakura: His Life and Works
13. Bābājī Mahārāja: Two Beyond Duality: Biographies of Their Divine Graces
14. Śrī Bhaktisiddhānta Vaibhava
15. Srila Prabhupada-lilamrta

PRAYERS (P)

1. Prema Bhakti Chandrika
2. Prarthana (Prayers)
3. Saranagati (Surrender)
4. Gita-mala (A Garland of Songs)
5. Gitavali (Song collection)
6. Kalyana Kalpataru
7. Stava-mala
8. Stavavali
9. Padyavali
10. Stavamrita Lahiri

PLACES (PL)

1. Govinda Vrindavanastakam
2. Vraja-riti-chintamani
3. Mathura Mahatmya
4. Mathura mandala Parikrama
5. Sri Vrindavana Mahimanrta
6. Sri Navadvipa Dhama Mahatmya
7. Navadvipa-sataka
8. Sri Sri Navadvipa Bhava Taranga
9. Jagannatha Mandir

PASTIMES (PS)

1. Gopala Campu
2. Vidagdha Madhava
3. Lalita Madhava
4. Dana Keli Kaumudi
5. Ananda Vrindavana Campu
6. Sri Krishna Vijaya
7. Sangeeta-madhava
8. Krsna Samhita
9. Camatkar Candrika
10. Krsna lila stava
11. Upakhyane Upadesa
12. Krsna, the Supreme Personality of Godhead

PERSONAL ESOTERIC PERSPECTIVE (PES)

1. Ujjvala Nilamani
2. Śrī Vilāpa Kusumāñjali
3. Govinda Lilamrita
4. Madhurya Kadambini
5. Raga Vartma Chandrika
6. Prakrita Rasa Shata Dushani
7. Brihad Vaishnava Toshani
8. Krishna-bhavanamrita
9. Hamsaduta
10. Uddhava Sandesha
11. Bhavana Sara Sangraha

12. Śrī Kṛṣṇa Karṇāmṛta
13. Śrī Gīta Govinda
14. Radha Rasa Sudha Nidhi
15. Prema Vivarta
16. Ujjvala Nilamani Kiranah
17. Sri Radhika Dhyanamrta

CHAPTER THREE

Introduction to Gaudiya Vaishnavism

Gaudiya Vaishnavism is a significant branch of Vaishnavism within Hinduism, emerged in 16th century Bengal, India, with the profound influence of **Lord Chaitanya Mahaprabhu** as its central figure. This period in India witnessed a vibrant socio-religious landscape, and Chaitanya's movement brought unique contributions by emphasizing intense devotion (bhakti) to Krishna,the Supreme Personality of Godhead. Following Chaitanya Mahaprabhu's disappearance, the Six Goswamis of Vrindavan played a pivotal role in systematically articulating and codifying the theological and philosophical underpinnings of this tradition. The rapid expansion and enduring impact of Gaudiya Vaishnavism suggest that its teachings resonated deeply with the spiritual aspirations of the time, providing a robust and compelling theological framework for its adherents.

Comparison to Indian Philosophical Systems

Within the vast landscape of Indian philosophical systems, Gaudiya Vaishnavism distinguishes itself primarily from the impersonalistic (Nirguna Brahman) schools like Advaita Vedanta by asserting the supreme personality of Godhead. While Advaita posits that the ultimate reality is an undifferentiated, attributeless Brahman and that the individual soul is identical with this Brahman, Gaudiya Vaishnavism maintains that the Supreme is always a person, Bhagavan Sri Krishna, who possesses infinite transcendental qualities, and that individual souls are eternal, distinct, though qualitatively one, parts of Him. Unlike the analytical dualism of Samkhya or the liberation-focused asceticism of classical Yoga (which often culminates in kaivalya or isolation of the purusha), Gaudiya Vaishnavism posits that the highest perfection is not simply liberation from material suffering, but active, loving service to the Supreme Lord in a personal relationship. It also contrasts with Mimamsa's focus on Vedic rituals for material benefits and Nyaya-Vaisheshika's emphasis on logic and atomism, by prioritizing the devotional path of bhakti-yoga and the chanting of the Holy Name as the most direct and potent means to spiritual realization in this age.

Philosophical Basis

At the heart of Gaudiya Vaishnava philosophy lies the principle of **Achintya Bheda Abheda**, which offers a detailed explanation of the simultaneous oneness and difference between God, specifically Krishna, and His creation. This includes the individual souls (jivas) and the material energy (prakriti). The scriptures of Gaudiya Vaishnavism employ various illustrative examples and analogies to elucidate this complex philosophical concept, making it more accessible to practitioners. Furthermore, this principle is carefully distinguished from other philosophical systems to prevent misunderstandings and highlight its unique contribution to understanding the nature of reality. This foundational principle likely serves as the bedrock upon which all other aspects of Gaudiya Vaishnava theology are built, profoundly influencing the understanding of devotion, liberation, and the very nature of existence. The concept of the jiva, or individual soul, is another crucial aspect of this philosophy. It posits that the soul is eternal, constituting a part and parcel of Krishna, possessing an inherent inclination towards rendering devotional service (bhakti). The soul's entanglement within the material world is attributed to a state of forgetfulness regarding its true identity and its relationship with Krishna. This emphasis on the soul's intrinsic connection to Krishna provides a theological rationale for the practice of bhakti, positioning it as the most natural and fulfilling activity for the individual. Complementing this understanding is the concept of Maya, often translated as illusion. Maya is explained as the illusory energy that obscures the soul's true knowledge and understanding. It exerts a powerful influence on perception, leading to the creation of a false sense of self and a distorted view of reality. The path of bhakti is presented as the primary means by which one can transcend the influence of Maya and attain true spiritual realization. Understanding the concept of Maya is therefore considered essential for practitioners, as it illuminates the fundamental cause of suffering and underscores the necessity of engaging in spiritual practices to overcome this illusion.

Krishna The Supreme Personality of Godhead

The theological framework of Gaudiya Vaishnavism places Krishna as the Supreme Personality of Godhead. This tradition offers a detailed exposition on Krishna as the original and ultimate form of God, recognized as the source from which all other incarnations and expansions emanate. Scriptural evidence drawn from revered texts such as the

Bhagavad Gita and Srimad Bhagavatam is frequently cited to support the supremacy of Krishna. These texts elaborate on the unique qualities and attributes of Krishna, including His unparalleled beauty, sweetness, and boundless compassion. Establishing Krishna as the supreme object of worship is fundamental to Gaudiya Vaishnavism, shaping the very nature and focus of devotional practices within the tradition. The emphasis on Krishna as the ultimate reality defines the core of its theological perspective. Alongside Krishna, **Radha/Srimati Radharani** occupies a central and unique position in Gaudiya Vaishnavism. She is revered as Krishna's eternal consort and is the very embodiment of divine love (prema). Radha is not merely a companion but holds the esteemed position of being Krishna's most beloved devotee and the principal source of His divine pleasure. The theological significance of the **Radha-Krishna relationship** is profound, as it is understood to represent the ultimate expression of divine love and serves as the quintessential model for the individual soul's relationship with God. This emphasis on Radha is a distinctive characteristic of Gaudiya Vaishnavism, highlighting the paramount importance of loving devotion and recognizing the significance of the feminine aspect of the divine in the pursuit of spiritual realization. While many other Vaishnava traditions primarily focus on Vishnu or Krishna, the prominent role accorded to Radha in Gaudiya Vaishnavism signifies a unique theological perspective on the nature of divine love and the intricate dynamics of the Godhead.

The Devotional Service

Gaudiya Vaishnavism emphasizes that devotional service, or bhakti, is the primary and most efficacious means of achieving love of God (prema), which is considered the ultimate aim of human life. This path of bhakti is presented as the most direct route to spiritual realization, particularly in contrast to other paths such as jnana-yoga (the path of knowledge) and karma-yoga (the path of action). ***Bhakti is described as being accessible and universal, open to all individuals irrespective of their social background, status, or qualifications.*** This prioritization of bhakti underscores the emotional and relational dimension of spirituality within Gaudiya Vaishnavism, making it potentially more approachable to a wider audience compared to more intellectually or ritually focused spiritual disciplines. The tradition outlines **a structured approach** to cultivating bhakti through **the nine processes of devotional service.**

These nine forms are: hearing (shravanam) about Krishna, chanting (kirtanam) His holy names and glories, remembering (vishnu-smaranam) Krishna, serving His lotus feet (pada-sevanam), offering formal worship (archanam), offering prayers (vandanam), acting as Krishna's servant (dasyam), cultivating friendship with Krishna (sakhyam), and completely surrendering oneself to Krishna (atma-nivedanam).

Scriptural references and illustrative examples are provided for each of these nine processes, offering practical guidance for devotees. This systematic framework for bhakti enables practitioners to engage in devotional activities in diverse ways, catering to their individual inclinations and capacities.

Sadhana - Regular Spiritual Practice

Furthermore, Gaudiya Vaishnavism places significant emphasis on the importance of sadhana, or regular spiritual practice, in cultivating bhakti and making progress on the spiritual path. Key sadhana practices include the chanting of the Hare Krishna mantra (both individually as japa and collectively as kirtan), the study of sacred scriptures, associating with other devotees (sanga), and residing in holy places associated with Krishna's pastimes. Consistent engagement in these spiritual practices is considered essential for overcoming material attachments and developing love for God, highlighting the active role that the devotee must take in their own spiritual journey. Spiritual realization, in this context, is understood not merely as an intellectual understanding but as a transformative process that requires dedicated effort and immersion in practices that purify the heart and mind.

The Key Scriptures

The theological and philosophical tenets of Gaudiya Vaishnavism are deeply rooted in a **collection of key scriptures,** each holding significant importance within the tradition. Among these, **the Bhagavad Gita** holds a foundational position, revered as a concise yet comprehensive summary of Vedic wisdom and the direct teachings of Krishna. The Gita addresses various key themes relevant to Gaudiya Vaishnavism, including the nature of the soul, the principles of karma, and the different paths of yoga, with a particular emphasis on the path of bhakti. Gaudiya Vaishnava scholars have produced numerous commentaries on the Bhagavad Gita, interpreting its verses through the lens of bhakti and highlighting Krishna's personal nature and the supremacy of devotional service as the means to attain Him. While the Bhagavad Gita is a widely respected scripture across many schools of Hindu thought, Gaudiya Vaishnavism's unique interpretation underscores its commitment to bhakti as the highest spiritual pursuit. **The Srimad Bhagavatam,** also known as the Bhagavata Purana, is considered the most important scripture within Gaudiya Vaishnavism. It elaborates extensively on the nature of Krishna, His devotees, and the intricate path of bhakti. The Bhagavatam contains detailed accounts of Krishna's divine pastimes (lila) and narrates the inspiring stories of numerous great devotees. It is often described within the tradition as the ripened fruit of Vedic knowledge, representing the most complete and authoritative exposition of its teachings. The Srimad Bhagavatam serves as the primary source for understanding the multifaceted nature of Krishna and the profound intricacies of bhakti-yoga. Following the advent of Chaitanya Mahaprabhu, the Six Goswamis of Vrindavan played a crucial role in systematically organizing and articulating the philosophy and theology of Gaudiya Vaishnavism. Their collective writings represent a significant intellectual and theological contribution, transforming the initially ecstatic expressions of Chaitanya's movement into a well-defined and coherent philosophical system. Key texts produced by the Goswamis include **the Sat Sandarbhas** by Jiva Goswami, which delve into the epistemology, ontology, and theology of the tradition, establishing its philosophical basis. Rupa Goswami authored the **Bhakti-rasamrita-sindhu**, which meticulously analyzes the science of devotional service, categorizing the different stages and flavors of bhakti, and the Ujjvala-nilamani, which focuses on the aesthetics of divine love, particularly the sublime relationship between Radha and Krishna, providing a model for the soul's ultimate aspiration. Gopala Bhatta Goswami contributed the **Hari-bhakti-vilasa**, which offers practical guidance on the rules and regulations for Gaudiya Vaishnava practice and worship, ensuring proper conduct and fostering devotion. The writings of each Goswami contributed uniquely to different aspects of the theology, encompassing epistemology, ontology, aesthetics, and practical application.

Guru-Spiritual teacher

Within Gaudiya Vaishnavism, great importance is placed on **the role of the guru, or spiritual teacher**, and the concept of disciplic succession, known as **parampara.** The tradition emphasizes the necessity of receiving guidance from a qualified spiritual teacher to make genuine progress on the path of bhakti. The guru serves as a guide, providing essential instruction, initiation into spiritual practices, and personal mentorship to the disciple. The scriptures themselves outline specific qualities that characterize a genuine and authentic guru. This strong emphasis on the guru highlights the recognition within Gaudiya Vaishnavism that the spiritual journey can be complex and challenging, necessitating personal guidance from someone who has already traversed the path and attained spiritual realization. The concept of disciplic succession, or parampara, further underscores the importance of authentic spiritual transmission. It refers to the unbroken chain of spiritual teachers and disciples that originates directly from Krishna Himself. Receiving knowledge and initiation through a legitimate parampara is considered essential for ensuring the authenticity and purity of the teachings.

Bhakti is a Lifestyle

The practical aspects of Gaudiya Vaishnavism are deeply integrated into the daily lives of its practitioners through a variety of prescribed practices and lifestyle guidelines. A typical **daily schedule** often includes dedicated time for chanting the Hare Krishna mantra, both as individual meditation (japa) and communal singing (kirtan). Prayer and the study of sacred scriptures also form an integral part of daily spiritual discipline, fostering a deeper understanding of the philosophical and theological principles. For many practitioners, deity worship (arcana) is another significant daily practice. The chanting of the Hare Krishna mantra is considered the primary spiritual practice for this age, believed to be the most effective means of purifying the heart and mind and awakening one's innate love for Krishna. The tradition also provides guidelines for maintaining a spiritual lifestyle, including specific **dietary regulations** that prohibit the consumption of meat, fish, and eggs. Ethical conduct, characterized by compassion, truthfulness, and non-violence, is also strongly emphasized as essential for spiritual progress. **The worship of the deity forms** of Krishna and Radha holds a central place in Gaudiya Vaishnavism, both in temples and in the homes of devotees. Detailed procedures are prescribed for offering prayers, food (which, after being offered to the deities, is known as prasadam), and other forms of service to the deities. The act of seeing and serving the deities is considered spiritually significant, fostering a tangible and personal connection with the divine. Gaudiya Vaishnavism also emphasizes the importance of celebrating key events in the lives of Krishna and Chaitanya Mahaprabhu through various festivals and holy days. **Major festivals** such as Janmashtami (the birth of Krishna), Radhashtami (the birth of Radha), and Gaura Purnima (the appearance day of Chaitanya Mahaprabhu) are observed with great enthusiasm and devotion. These celebrations often involve special **prayers, chanting, fasting, and discourses** on the lives and teachings of Krishna and Chaitanya. **Visiting holy places,** particularly **Vrindavan** (where Krishna spent His childhood) and

Mayapur (the birthplace of Chaitanya Mahaprabhu), is also considered highly auspicious and an important aspect of spiritual practice within the tradition. Communal celebrations and **pilgrimages** to these sacred sites serve to strengthen the spiritual community and provide opportunities for intensified devotional engagement.

Attaining Prema-The ultimate goal

The ultimate aim of life in Gaudiya Vaishnavism is to attain prema-bhakti, or pure, selfless love for Krishna. Prema is described as a transcendental emotion that transcends other forms of love and material attachment. It is considered the highest form of spiritual realization and the natural culmination of the path of bhakti. The tradition outlines various stages of bhakti that gradually lead to the development of prema. This emphasis on prema highlights the deeply personal and loving relationship that the individual soul can cultivate with God, going beyond mere intellectual comprehension or ritualistic performance. The experience of prema is often described in terms of ecstatic symptoms and profound transcendental emotions. The liberation (moksha) attained through prema is understood not simply as freedom from material suffering but as **the positive experience of eternal bliss in loving service to Krishna.** This vision of the ultimate spiritual fulfillment serves as a powerful motivation for practitioners to diligently pursue the highest state of devotion. Ultimately, the highest expression of prema is understood as participation in the eternal loving pastimes of Radha and Krishna in the spiritual world of Vrindavan. Devotees aspire to serve the Divine Couple in one of the various rasas, or divine relationships, such as servitude, friendship, parental affection, or conjugal love. This ultimate aspiration provides a specific and deeply personal understanding of

the final destination of the soul, emphasizing the eternal nature of the loving relationship with the Divine Couple in the spiritual realm.

Global stage and Gaudiya Vaishnavism

While not always at the forefront of mainstream Western philosophical discourse, growing international presence and the depth of its intellectual and spiritual heritage position Gaudiya Vaishnavism as a significant voice in the ongoing dialogue about the nature of reality, consciousness, and the human pursuit of meaning and happiness.

Comparison to Other Philosophical Systems of the World

When compared to other philosophical systems across the globe, Gaudiya Vaishnavism stands out due to its unique emphasis on a personal, loving, and supremely attractive Godhead (Radha and Krishna), and the ultimate goal of developing prema-bhakti (pure divine love) rather than mere liberation or intellectual understanding. While many Western philosophies, for instance, often prioritize logic, reason, and empirical observation in their quest for truth, Gaudiya Vaishnavism grounds its epistemology in revealed scripture and the experience of divine love. Unlike Abrahamic religions, which also feature a personal God, Gaudiya Vaishnavism presents a nuanced understanding of divine relationships, advocating for five primary rasas (mellows of love) culminating in the intimate conjugal love (madhurya-rasa) exemplified by Radha and Krishna. Furthermore, its Achintya Bheda Abheda Tattva provides a distinct reconciliation of oneness and difference that offers a unique perspective on the absolute truth, differing from both strict monotheism and pantheism.

In terms of credentials, Gaudiya Vaishnavism boasts a rich scriptural basis rooted in the Vedas, Upanishads, Bhagavad-gita, and especially the Srimad Bhagavatam (Bhagavata Purana), which it considers the ripened fruit of Vedic wisdom. It presents a sophisticated metaphysical understanding of the relationship between God (Krishna), the individual soul (jiva), and the material world, articulated through the principle of achintya-bheda-abheda tattva – inconceivable simultaneous oneness and difference. This nuanced philosophy distinguishes it from both strict monism and dualism, offering a unique perspective on ontology.

The Gaudiya tradition possesses a well-developed epistemology, emphasizing scriptural authority (shabda-pramana), realized understanding through devotional practice, and the guidance of qualified spiritual teachers in a disciplic succession (parampara). Its ethical framework is deeply embedded in the principles of bhakti-yoga, emphasizing compassion, non-violence, truthfulness, and a life dedicated to the service of God and all beings.

Furthermore, Gaudiya Vaishnavism offers a highly refined aesthetic and experiential dimension through its detailed understanding of rasa (divine mellows) and the cultivation of loving devotion (prema) as the ultimate goal of life. The tradition's rich artistic expressions in music (kirtan), dance, literature, and temple art contribute to its unique cultural and philosophical footprint globally.Gaudiya Vaishnavism holds a significant, albeit sometimes niche, position on the global philosophy stage, offering a unique and comprehensive theological system with distinct credentials. Its global presence has been largely facilitated by the **International Society for Krishna Consciousness (ISKCON),** founded by A.C. Bhaktivedanta

Swami Prabhupada in the mid-20th century, which successfully transplanted this tradition to the West and beyond.

The foundational books of Gaudiya Vaishnavism present a comprehensive and intricate system of theology, philosophy, and practice centered on the supreme worship of Radha and Krishna. This tradition offers unique contributions to Vaishnavism and Hindu philosophy through its emphasis on Achintya Bheda Abheda, the centrality of Radha, the preeminence of bhakti-yoga, and the detailed understanding of prema as the ultimate spiritual goal. **The teachings found within these scriptures continue to hold significance and relevance in the contemporary world, providing a profound path of spiritual realization for those seeking a deeper connection with the Divine.**Let's explore the foundational scriptures of Gaudiya Vaishnavism!

CHAPTER FOUR

Why to read Scriptures?

Reading Gaudiya Vaishnava books and especially Srila Prabhupada books offers a wealth of spiritual, intellectual, and personal benefits. Here's why they are so valuable:

1. Access to Authentic Vedic Wisdom:

- **Unadulterated Knowledge:** These books present the ancient Vedic scriptures which are in sanskrit and difficult to understand, such as the *Bhagavad-gita* and *Srimad-Bhagavatam*, "as they are," without personal interpretations or adulterations. This provides a direct connection to the original wisdom.They are **SHABD PRAMAN !**

- **Clarity and Authority:** His translations and commentaries are renowned for their clarity, depth, and fidelity to the original texts and the Gaudiya Vaishnava tradition. Scholars worldwide appreciate their authoritative presentation.

2. Profound Understanding of Life and Reality:

1. **Answers to Fundamental Questions:** These books delve into the essential questions of life: Who am I? What is the purpose of life? What is the nature of the universe? What happens after death?
2. **Understanding Our Eternal Nature:** They explain that we are eternal spiritual beings, distinct from our temporary material bodies, offering a profound sense of identity and purpose.
3. **Knowledge of the Material and Spiritual Worlds:** Prabhupada's works provide detailed insights into the workings of the material world, the laws of karma, and the nature of the spiritual realm.

3. Practical Guidance for Spiritual Growth:

- **The Science of Bhakti-yoga:** The books meticulously explain the principles and practices of Bhakti-yoga, the path of loving devotion to the Supreme Person, Krishna.
- **Step-by-Step Instructions:** They offer practical guidance on how to cultivate a spiritual life through chanting, meditation, deity worship, and following a conscious lifestyle.
- **The Importance of a Spiritual Master:** Srila Prabhupada emphasizes the crucial role of a genuine spiritual guide in navigating the spiritual path.

4. Personal Transformation and Well-being:

- **Overcoming Suffering:** By understanding the temporary nature of material existence and our eternal spiritual identity, readers can gain perspective and learn to transcend suffering.

- **Finding Inner Peace and Happiness:** The practice of Bhakti-yoga, as outlined in these books, leads to inner peace, contentment, and a deeper connection with the Divine source of all happiness.
- **Developing Positive Qualities:** Reading and applying these teachings can foster compassion, humility, tolerance, and other virtuous qualities.

5. Connection with a Global Spiritual Community:

- **Foundation of ISKCON:** Srila Prabhupada's books are the foundational literature of the International Society for Krishna Consciousness (ISKCON), connecting readers to a worldwide community of practitioners.
- **Inspiration and Guidance:** They serve as a constant source of inspiration and guidance for millions seeking spiritual fulfillment.

6. Legacy of a Pure Devotee:

- **Association with Srila Prabhupada:** Reading his books is considered a powerful way to associate with Srila Prabhupada, a pure devotee of Krishna, even in his physical absence.
- **His Personal Touch:** All of us feel a direct connection and guidance from Srila Prabhupada through his words.In essence, reading Vaishnava books and especially Srila Prabhupada's books offers a comprehensive education in spiritual science, providing both the theoretical knowledge and the practical means to achieve a fulfilling and meaningful life, ultimately leading to self-realization and love of God.

CHAPTER FIVE

Gaudiya Vaishnava Literature: An Overview

1. Foundational Seeds in Early Texts:

Śrī Śikṣāṣṭakam: These eight verses by Sri Chaitanya Mahaprabhu himself are the foundational heart of the entire theology. They encapsulate the essence of bhakti — the chanting of the holy name, humility, detachment, and the longing for divine love. All subsequent philosophical developments aim to explain and elaborate on these core principles.

ārādhyo bhagavān vrajeśa-tanayas tad-dhāma
vṛndāvanaṁ
ramyā kācid upāsanā vraja-vadhū-vargeṇa yā kalpitā |
śāstraṁ bhāgavatam pramāṇam amalaṁ premā
pumārtho mahān
itthaṁ gaura-mahāprabhor matam atas tatrādaro naḥ
paraḥ ||

(Caitanya-mata-mañjuṣā: 1.1)

"'*The object of worship is Bhagavān, the Son of Vraja's king. His abode is Vṛndāvana. The lovely worship [that is to be performed] is that which is performed by the ladies of Vraja. The flawless pramāṇa [i.e., means of knowing these conclusions] is the śāstra [Śrīmad] Bhāgavatam, and the [rightful ultimate] aim of a human being is prema.' This is the view of Gaura Mahāprabhu, and thus we have the highest regard for it.*"

Śrī Kṛṣṇa-karṇāmṛta & Śrī Gīta-govinda: These earlier devotional poems, while not strictly Gaudiya philosophical treatises, deeply influenced the Gaudiya understanding of the sweetness (madhurya) of Krishna's pastimes and the intense emotions of love for Him, particularly the love of the gopis. They set a devotional tone and provided rich subject matter for later philosophical analysis.

2. The Goswamis of Vrindavan: Systematization and Elaboration:

i) Rupa Goswami's Contribution:

Bhakti-rasamrita-sindhu: This monumental work systematically categorizes and analyzes the science of bhakti-rasa (the taste of devotional love), providing a comprehensive framework for understanding the different stages and types of devotion. It establishes the supremacy of madhurya-rasa.

Ujjvala-nilamani: Building upon Bhakti-rasamrita-sindhu, this text specifically and meticulously analyzes ujjvala-rasa (conjugal love), the highest form of bhakti, providing detailed descriptions of the nayikas (heroines), nayaka (hero – Krishna), and the various emotional states involved.

Laghu-bhagavatamrita: This offers a concise overview of the Lord and His devotees, establishing the hierarchical relationships within the spiritual world and the importance of the Bhagavata Purana.

His other works like**Upadesamrita,Vidagdha-madhava,Lalita-madhava,Hamsaduta,Uddhava Sandesha,Padyavali**further illustrate the intense devotional emotions that form the subject of his philosophical analyses.

<u>ii) Sanatana Goswami's Contribution:</u>

Brihad-bhagavatamrita: This expansive work narrates the journeys of a spiritual seeker, exploring the glories of various devotees and the different levels of the spiritual realm, ultimately establishing the supremacy of Krishna and Vrindavan. It emphasizes the importance of bhagavata (devotees and scripture).

Hari-bhakti-vilasa: While focusing on sadhana (devotional practice) and rituals, this book is deeply rooted in theological principles, outlining the proper conduct and understanding for devotees.

other books **Krishna-lila-stava,Brihad Vaishnava Toshani are also important contribution to Gaudiya Parampara.**

<u>iii) Raghunatha Dasa Goswami's contribution</u>

He is known for his intense renunciation and deep devotion. His significant literary contributions include:**Vilapa Kusumanjali** (A Lamentation in the Form of a Shower of Flowers) - A collection of prayers expressing intense yearning and lamentation for the mercy of Sri Sri Radha and Krishna and their eternal associates.

His other works are **Stavavali (A Necklace of Prayers),Dana-keli-cintamani,Gauḍa-stava-kalpataru,Sri**

Sri Radha-Krishna Uddipa-na Satakam,Manaḥ-śikṣā

iv)Srila Gopala Bhatta Goswami's contribution

He is known for his significant contributions to Gaudiya Vaishnava literature and the establishment of Deity worship. His prominent works include:**Sat-kriya-Sara-dipika** (Lamp for the Essence of Proper Actions) - A manual on Vaishnava samskaras (rites of passage) and rituals, guiding devotees through various life events from birth to death according to Vaishnava principles.

Hari-bhakti-vilasa (Performance of Devotion to Hari) - While often attributed to Sanatana Goswami (as he edited and presented it), it is considered that Gopala Bhatta Goswami compiled the bulk of the material for this extensive guide on Vaishnava smriti (rules and regulations) and devotional practices.

His other works are **Karma-smriti ,Sri Krishna-vallabha ,Laghu Hari-bhakti-vilasa**

v) Jiva Goswami's Contribution:

Sat Sandarbhas: These six treatises form the philosophical bedrock of Gaudiya Vaishnavism. They systematically establish the metaphysics (nature of God, soul, and world), epistemology (sources of knowledge), and soteriology (path to liberation and divine love) of the tradition, drawing heavily from scripture and the works of Rupa and Sanatana.

Gopala Campu: This unique work blends poetic narrative with philosophical exposition, vividly portraying Krishna's Vrindavan pastimes while subtly weaving in profound theological insights.

Sarva-samvadini and his commentaries serve to further clarify and defend the philosophical conclusions presented in the Sandarbhas.

Other important works are **Gopala-virudavali,Madhava-mahotsava,Sankalpa-kalpadruma,Harinamāmṛta-vyākaraṇam,Sūtra-mālikā,Dhatu-sangraha,Brahma-Samhita commentary**

vi) Srila Raghunatha Bhatta Goswami Historical records indicate that unlike the other Goswamis, he did not write any books. He was primarily known for his exceptional recitation and explanation of the Srimad-Bhagavatam, his melodious kirtans, and his strict adherence to Vaishnava principles. His service was focused on hearing and chanting, and inspiring others through his personal example and powerful spoken word.

3. The Role of Commentaries and Later Acharyas:

Vishvanatha Chakravarti Thakur: His commentaries, such as **Sarartha Darshini** on the Bhagavatam and **Sarartha-varshini** on the Gita, made the complex philosophical ideas of the Goswamis more accessible while also offering his own insightful interpretations and elaborations, particularly on the nuances of rasa. His independent works like **Madhurya Kadambini and Raga Vartma Chandrika** further explored the path of devotion.

Baladeva Vidyabhushana: His Govinda Bhashya provided the Gaudiya school with its own commentary on the Vedanta Sutra, firmly establishing its Vedantic credentials while maintaining its distinct theological perspective centered on the personal Godhead, Krishna. His other works like **Prameya Ratnavali and Tattva Sandarbha Tika** (commentary on Jiva Goswami's first Sandarbha) further solidified the philosophical system.

4. The Bhakti Renaissance of the Late 19ᵗʰ and Early 20ᵗʰ Centuries:

Bhaktivinoda Thakur: He played a crucial role in reviving and systematizing Gaudiya Vaishnavism in modern times. He was a prolific writer and spiritual visionary who authored over **one hundred books** in **Sanskrit, Bengali, and English,** profoundly shaping the modern Gaudiya Vaishnava movement. Among his most influential works are **Jaiva Dharma**, a seminal philosophical novel presenting Vaishnava theology through narrative; **Harinama Cintamani,** which delves into the philosophy and practice of chanting the Holy Name; and devotional songbooks such as **Gitavali, Saranagati, and Kalyana Kalpataru,** filled with heartfelt prayers and philosophical insights. Other significant contributions include **Tattva Viveka, Datta Kaustubha, and Tattva Sutra,** which systematically explain Vaishnava philosophy; **Bhagavatarka Marichi Mala,** a compilation of verses from the Srimad-Bhagavatam; and educational texts like **Sri Chaitanya-sikshamrita and Sri Chaitanya Mahaprabhur Shiksha,** summarizing the teachings of Sri Chaitanya Mahaprabhu. His extensive literary output laid a strong foundation for the global propagation of Gaudiya Vaishnavism.

Bhaktisiddhanta Sarasvati Thakur: He further propagated the teachings of Chaitanya Mahaprabhu and established the Gaudiya Math. Key among his works are his profound commentaries, such as **the Gaudiya Bhashya** on the Srimad-Bhagavatam, **the Anubhashya** on the Chaitanya Charitamrita, and his insightful **elucidation of the Brahma-Samhita.** He also compiled and published numerous ancient texts, including the works of the Six Goswamis and other foundational scriptures, making them accessible to a wider audience. Furthermore, his philosophical essays and articles, many of which appeared in his journals like The **Harmonist (Sajjana-toshani)**, provided rigorous analytical discussions on various theological and devotional topics, firmly establishing the siddhanta (conclusive truths) of the Gaudiya Vaishnava tradition.His commentaries and essays often focused on the purity of devotional practice and the refutation of materialistic interpretations, emphasizing the absolute nature of the spiritual reality.

5. *The Global Expansion and Continued Elaboration*

A.C. Bhaktivedanta Swami Prabhupada His translations and **commentaries on key texts** like the Bhagavad-gita, Srimad Bhagavatam, and Chaitanya Charitamrita made the Gaudiya Vaishnava philosophy accessible to a worldwide audience. His purports often provide clear and practical applications of the complex theological concepts. His summary works like The Nectar of Devotion and The Nectar of Instruction serve as excellent introductions to the core principles derived from the Goswamis' teachings.

Evolution and Revelation:

The philosophy wasn't revealed in a single moment but unfolded through the inspired writings and realizations of successive generations of acharyas.

Sriman Chaitanya Mahaprabhu provided the experiential and foundational principles.

The Goswamis systematically articulated and philosophically grounded these principles, drawing deeply from scripture and their own profound realizations. They provided the detailed structure and vocabulary of Gaudiya theology.

Later commentators and acharyas clarified, defended, and applied these principles in different contexts, making them more accessible and relevant to their times. They built upon the foundation laid by the Goswamis, further illuminating the nuances and complexities of the tradition.

In essence, there's a clear lineage of thought, with each subsequent generation building upon the insights of their predecessors. **The early devotional outpourings provided the heart, the Goswamis the intellectual framework, and the later acharyas the clarification and practical application, leading to the rich and comprehensive theological system that is Gaudiya Vaishnavism today.**

• 35 •

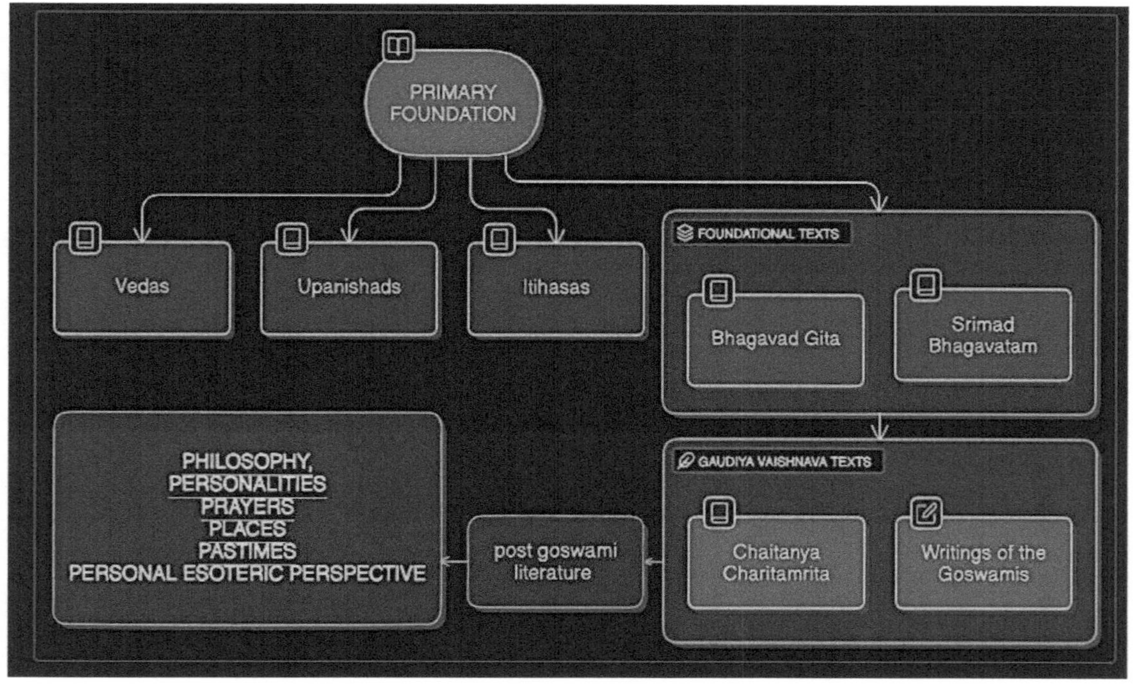

BOOKS CLASSIFICATION

• 37 •

CHAPTER SIX

How to read?

To deepen your understanding and appreciation of teachings, here are some tips for reading books:

1. Start with the Foundational books :

- **Bhagavad-gita As It Is:** This is considered the entry point and provides the foundational philosophy of Krishna Consciousness. Read the introduction carefully as it sets the context.
- **Science of Self-Realization:** A collection of lectures and essays that further explain the basic principles.This is the best book in my opinion which should be regularly read by all the devotees in all stage of life.

2. Gradual Progression in foundational books :

1. **Category 1 Books:** After the essentials, move on to other introductory books like *On the Way to Krishna, Elevation to Krishna Consciousness, Krishna Consciousness: The Matchless Gift, Krishna: The Reservoir of Pleasure, Easy Journey to Other Planets,Perfection of Yoga, Beyond Birth and Death, Perfect Questions, Perfect Answers, Raja-Vidya: The King of Knowledge, The Nectar of Instruction,* and *Teachings of Queen Kunti.* These build

a solid philosophical base.

2. **Category 2 Books:** Once you have a good grasp of the basics, you can delve into books like *Teachings of Lord Kapila, Sri Isopanisad,* the *Krishna Book* (summary study of the Tenth Canto of Srimad-Bhagavatam), and the First Canto of *Srimad-Bhagavatam.*

3. **Category 3 Books:** Finally, you can undertake the more extensive works: *Srimad-Bhagavatam* (canto by canto), *The Nectar of Devotion* (Bhakti-rasamrita-sindhu), and *Sri Caitanya-caritamrita.*

3. Approach with Reverence and a Learning Attitude:

- **Sacred Space:** Find a quiet place where you can read without interruption.
- **Humble Attitude:** Approach the books with a genuine desire to learn and receive guidance.
- **Offer Prayers:** Before reading, you can offer a prayer to Srila Prabhupada and Lord Krishna to help you understand the material.

4. Engage Deeply with the Text:

- **Read Slowly:** Focus on understanding the meaning rather than just covering a certain number of pages.
- **Pay Attention to Detail:** Srila Prabhupada's purports (commentaries) are rich with explanations and insights. *Read them carefully.*
- **Reflect and Meditate:** When a particular point or word strikes you, pause and contemplate its meaning and relevance to your life.
- **Look Up References:** Srila Prabhupada often quotes Vedic scriptures. If possible, refer to these original texts

for a deeper understanding.

5. Reinforce Your Understanding:

- **Discuss with Others:** Share your realizations and insights with fellow devotees. This helps you understand the teachings from different perspectives.
- **Listen to Lectures:** Complement your reading by listening to Srila Prabhupada's lectures on the same topics. Hearing the message can provide further clarity.
- **Apply the Teachings:** The ultimate aim is to integrate these teachings into your daily life. Try to apply the principles you learn in your thoughts, words, and actions.
- **Read Regularly:** Srila Prabhupada emphasized the importance of daily reading for spiritual advancement. Even reading a little every day can make a significant difference.

6. Seek Guidance:

- **Senior Devotees:** If you have questions or find certain concepts difficult to understand, don't hesitate to ask more experienced devotees for clarification.

By following these tips, you can make your reading of Srila Prabhupada's books a transformative and enriching experience, guiding you on your journey of spiritual realization.

Three Categories of Foundational books

(as guided by HH Bhakti Rasamrit Maharaj)

CATEGORY I
01. On The Way to Krishna
02. Elevation to Krishna Consciousness
03. Krishna Consciousness the Matchless Gift
04. Krishna the Reservoir of Pleasure
05. Perfection of Yoga
06. Krishna Consciousness – The Topmost Yoga System
07. Beyond Birth and Death
08. Perfect Questions, Perfect Answers
09. Easy Journey to Other Planets
10. Raja Vidya: The King of Knowledge
11. Transcendental Teachings of Prahlad Maharaj
12. Coming Back
13. Message of Godhead
14. Civilization and Transcendence
15. Hare Krishna Challenge
16. Scientific Basis of Krishna Consciousness*
17. Sword of Knowledge
18. Nectar of Instruction
19. Path of Perfection
20. Issues of Back To Back to Godhead Magazine
21. Prabhupada Lilamrita
CATEGORY II
These books are to be read after one has completed all books in category I
01. Bhagvad Gita As It Is as overview
02. Science of Self-Realization
03. Journey of Self Discovery

04. Life comes from Life

05. Nectar of Devotion (Only Part One)

06. Teachings of Queen Kunti

07. Teachings of Lord Kapila

08. Teachings of Lord Chaitanya

09. Sri Isopanishad

10. Few Shlokas of Bhagvad Gita Everyday

11. Krishna Book

12. Srimad Bhagavatam (1st Canto)

13. A Second Chance

CATEGORY III

These books are to be read after one has completed all books in category I and category II

01. Bhagvad Gita As It Is - more deeper study 'Basics of Bhagavad gita' by BBT is very helpful

02. Srimad Bhagavatam (Canto By Canto)

03. Nectar Of Devotion (Part II And Part III)

04. Chaitanya Charitamrita

<u>Once you have become familiar with the above books, you may then commence reading additional books under the guidance of senior devotees. A list of 108 such books is presented in the next chapter and subsequently elaborated upon further in this book.</u>

CHAPTER SEVEN

108 Books Summary

The philosophical and theological depth of Gaudiya Vaishnavism is richly represented in its vast literary tradition. The foundational scriptures, along with the extensive writings of subsequent acharyas, and the contributions of Srila Prabhupada and his disciples offer profound insights into the nature of God, the soul, the material world, and the path of devotional service. The biographies provide inspiring accounts of the lives and teachings of key figures in the tradition. The texts summarized in this report, while not exhaustive of all important works, provide a comprehensive overview of the key philosophical concepts and devotional practices within the Gaudiya Vaishnava tradition. Further study of these and related texts will undoubtedly lead to a deeper appreciation of this rich and intricate spiritual system.

The selection of these 108 books was guided by a desire to present a comprehensive yet manageable overview of the foundational and highly influential texts within the Gaudiya Vaishnava tradition. The process involved several key considerations:

Authority and Lineage: Primary emphasis was placed on the writings of the Six Goswamis of Vrindavan (Rupa, Sanatana, Jiva, Gopala Bhatta, Raghunatha Dasa, and

Raghunatha Bhatta), who were directly commissioned by Sri Chaitanya Mahaprabhu to establish the philosophical and theological framework of the tradition. Their works are considered the cornerstone of Gaudiya Vaishnava thought.

Philosophical Foundation: Key texts that systematically present the core philosophical tenets of achintya-bhedabheda (inconceivable simultaneous oneness and difference), the nature of the Supreme Personality of Godhead (Krishna), the individual soul, maya (illusion), and the process of bhakti-yoga (devotional service) were prioritized. This includes the Sat-sandarbhas of Jiva Goswami and the foundational works of Rupa and Sanatana Goswamis.

Devotional Practice and Etiquette: Books outlining the principles and practices of sadhana-bhakti (regulated devotional practice), deity worship, Vaishnava etiquette, and the importance of the holy name were included. Hari-bhakti-vilasa and Upadeshamrita are prime examples of texts fulfilling this criterion.

Biographies and Narratives: Important biographical accounts of Sri Chaitanya Mahaprabhu and his close associates, such as Chaitanya Charitamrita, Chaitanya Bhagavata, and early biographies, were deemed essential for understanding the historical and emotional context of the tradition.

Poetic and Devotional Outpourings: The selection also incorporated significant collections of devotional songs (bhajans and stavas) and poetic works that express the deep love and longing for Krishna and Radha, exemplified by the writings of the Six Goswamis, Narottama Dasa Thakura, and others.

Commentaries and Elaborations: While the focus was primarily on the early and foundational texts, some influential commentaries by later acharyas like Vishvanatha Chakravarti Thakura and Baladeva Vidyabhushana were considered to represent significant developments and clarifications within the tradition.

Practical Guidance for Devotees: Texts offering practical instructions and encouragement for those pursuing the path of bhakti, such as Upadeshamrita and selected stavas, were included to provide relatable insights for contemporary practitioners.

Representing Key Authors: An effort was made to include at least one or more significant works from the most prominent acharyas throughout the history of the Gaudiya Vaishnava tradition, ensuring a representation of the evolution and richness of its literary heritage.

Avoiding Repetition (where possible in a summary): While many texts touch upon similar themes, preference was given to those that offer a unique perspective or a more in-depth treatment of a particular aspect of the philosophy or practice.

It is important to acknowledge that the selection of any finite number of books from a vast tradition involves a degree of selectivity. However, the aim here was to curate a collection that provides a solid foundation for understanding the core tenets, practices, and historical development of Gaudiya Vaishnavism, offering a valuable starting point for further exploration.

For further information and important shlokas of books mentioned in this compendium, visit Harigopinath Das website https://harigopinathdas.com/

108 Books

PRIMARY FOUNDATION

"Bhagavad-gītā is called the king of education because it is the essence of all doctrines and philosophies So there is no dearth of knowledge in the field of philosophy or transcendental knowledge. of all knowledge that can be derived from the study of the Vedas and different kinds of philosophy"

-Srila Prabhupada Bhagavad Gita as it is 9.2

The foundational texts of Gaudiya Vaishnavism are primarily the Vedic scriptures, with special emphasis on the Bhagavad-gita and the Srimad-Bhagavatam (also known as the Bhagavata Purana). The Srimad-Bhagavatam is considered the natural commentary on the Vedanta-sutra and the mature fruit of the Vedic tree of knowledge, elaborating extensively on the pastimes of Krishna and the science of bhakti. In addition to these, the writings of the Goswamis of Vrindavan (like Rupa Goswami, Sanatana Goswami, Jiva Goswami, etc.), who were direct disciples of Chaitanya Mahaprabhu, form a crucial part of the doctrinal and philosophical foundation. Their extensive literary contributions, including Bhakti-rasamrita-sindhu, Hari-bhakti-vilasa, and Jiva Goswami's Sat Sandarbhas, meticulously outline the philosophy, practices, and ultimate goals of the tradition.

1) Foundational texts

i) VEDAS-Four vedas

In Gaudiya Vaishnavism, the Vedas hold a position of paramount importance as the **ultimate source of revealed truth (*śruti*)**. Gaudiya Vaishnavism belongs to the Vedanta school of Hindu philosophy, which is based on the Upanishads and the Brahma-sutras.However, it offers its own unique interpretation, known as **Acintya-bhedābheda-tattva** ("inconceivable, simultaneous oneness and difference"), as propounded by Sri Chaitanya Mahaprabhu.Gaudiya Vaishnavism belongs to the Brahma-Madhva-Gaudiya Sampradaya, tracing its spiritual lineage back to Lord Brahma, then through Madhvacharya, and eventually to Sri Chaitanya Mahaprabhu. This lineage is crucial for establishing the authenticity and Vedic validity of its teachings. This philosophy reconciles the seemingly contradictory statements of the Vedas regarding the nature of God and the living entities (whether they are one with or different from God). It asserts that God (Krishna) is simultaneously one with His creation (qualitatively) and distinct from it (quantitatively).While the tradition places a special emphasis on the *Bhāgavata Purāṇa* (Śrīmad-Bhāgavatam) and the teachings of Śrī Caitanya Mahāprabhu, it firmly roots itself in the vast body of Vedic literature.

ii) UPANSIHAD-10 principle Upanishads

The ten principal Upanishads, collectively known as Dashopanishad, are Isha, Kena, Katha, Prashna, Mundaka, Mandukya, Taittiriya, Aitareya, Chandogya, and Brihadaranyaka.

iii) ITIHAS –Ramayana and Mahabharata

2) Siksastakam (Eight Instructions)

Author: Sri Chaitanya Mahaprabhu

- **Chaitanya Mahaprabhu's Sole Written Teaching:** The Siksastakam comprises the only eight verses directly penned by Sri Chaitanya Mahaprabhu Himself. While His life and teachings are extensively documented in various biographies (like Chaitanya Charitamrita), these eight verses are considered His direct, concise, and complete philosophical and practical instruction.
- **Essence of Chanting the Holy Name:** The Siksastakam is primarily a profound guide to the practice and realization of *hari-nama-sankirtana* (congregational chanting of the Holy Names of Krishna). The very first verse glorifies the Holy Name as the cleanser of the heart and the supreme benediction for humanity in the

Kali-yuga.

- **Progression of Devotional Experience:** The verses systematically outline the progressive stages of chanting and devotional experience, from cleansing the heart and extinguishing material desires to tasting transcendental bliss, realizing Krishna's name, form, qualities, and pastimes, and ultimately attaining pure love for Krishna.

- **Embodiment of Humility and Tolerance:** A central theme, especially in the third verse (*trinad api sunicena*), is the importance of cultivating extreme humility, tolerance, and respect for all living entities as prerequisites for truly benefiting from chanting the Holy Name. This principle is fundamental to Gaudiya Vaishnava practice.

- **Blueprint for Pure Love (Prema):** The Siksastakam beautifully describes the symptoms and internal feelings of a devotee in pure love for Krishna, culminating in the mood of separation from Krishna and Radharani, characterized by intense longing and yearning (*viraha*). It presents the highest aspiration of Gaudiya Vaishnavism – the spontaneous, pure love for Radha and Krishna as exemplified by the residents of Vrindavan.

3) Bhagavad Gita as it is

Author: Srila Prabhupada

- **Authentic Translation and Commentary:** It is a widely acclaimed and authoritative translation of the Bhagavad-gita, accompanied by extensive purports (commentaries) that present the verses "as they are," without speculative interpretations, but strictly in line with the Gaudiya Vaishnava tradition of Chaitanya Mahaprabhu.
- **Emphasis on Krishna as the Supreme Personality of Godhead:** A central theme is the clear presentation of Lord Krishna as the Supreme Personality of Godhead, the ultimate source of all existence, and the ultimate object of worship, rather than a mere historical figure or a symbol.
- **Stress on Bhakti-yoga (Devotional Service):** While covering karma-yoga (action), jnana-yoga (knowledge), and dhyana-yoga (meditation), the book culminates in the glorification of *bhakti-yoga* (devotional service) as the highest and most effective path to self-realization and God-realization, especially in the current age of Kali.
- **Practical Application of Spiritual Principles:** Prabhupada's purports are renowned for their practical advice, showing how the timeless wisdom of the Gita can be applied to modern life, addressing common doubts, challenges, and misconceptions.
- **Exposition of the Soul's Eternal Nature:** It clearly explains the distinction between the temporary material body and the eternal spiritual soul, emphasizing the soul's immutable nature and its eternal relationship with God.
- **Guidance on Detachment and Renunciation:** The book elaborates on the concept of selfless action (*karma-yoga*) and true renunciation, teaching how to act

without attachment to the fruits of labor, dedicating all efforts to the satisfaction of the Supreme Lord.

- **Exploration of the Three Modes of Material Nature:** It thoroughly describes the three *gunas* (modes of material nature – goodness, passion, and ignorance) and how they influence living entities, guiding the reader on how to transcend them for spiritual advancement.
- **The Importance of a Spiritual Master:** It underscores the necessity of approaching a genuine spiritual master in disciplic succession to properly understand and apply the teachings of the Bhagavad-gita, as Krishna's message is revealed through such a lineage.
- **Global Impact and Accessibility:** Published in over 80 languages, "Bhagavad-gita As It Is" has introduced millions worldwide to the wisdom of the Bhagavad-gita and the principles of Krishna consciousness, making it a foundational text for ISKCON and a widely respected academic resource.
- **A Call to Surrender (Sarva-dharman parityajya):** Ultimately, the book culminates in Krishna's direct instruction to Arjuna to surrender completely to Him, assuring him of protection from all sinful reactions. Prabhupada's purports consistently emphasize this ultimate conclusion of the Gita.

4) The Nectar of Instruction

(Upadesamrta by Srila Rupa Goswami, with purports by Srila Prabhupada)

Srila Prabhupada's "The Nectar of Instruction" is pivotal for practical spiritual advancement, offering a concise yet profound guide to cultivating pure devotional service. His purports illuminate Srila Rupa Goswami's original Sanskrit verses, providing essential instructions on controlling the senses and mind, identifying true spiritual association, and avoiding the six impediments to devotion. Its importance lies in presenting a step-by-step roadmap for sincerity and purification, making it an indispensable manual for aspiring devotees to navigate the complexities of spiritual life and progress towards Krishna consciousness.

5) The Nectar of Devotion

(Bhakti-rasamrta-sindhu by Srila Rupa Goswami, with purports by Srila Prabhupada)

"The Nectar of Devotion" is a cornerstone of Gaudiya Vaishnava philosophy, as Srila Prabhupada's illuminating purports to Srila Rupa Goswami's *Bhakti-rasamrta-sindhu* systematically reveal the complete science of *bhakti-yoga*. This book meticulously defines pure devotional service, categorizes its various stages and symptoms, and describes the different types of *rasas* (transcendental mellows) experienced in relationship with the Supreme Lord. Its importance lies in providing a comprehensive, authoritative, and practical guide for understanding the nature of devotion, enabling sincere practitioners to cultivate pure love for Krishna and appreciate the profound beauty of the spiritual world.

6) Sri Isopanisad (with purports by Srila Prabhupada)

"Sri Isopanisad" is a foundational Vedic scripture presented by Srila Prabhupada with purports that uniquely bridge the gap between impersonal Vedic wisdom and personalistic devotional understanding. Through its eighteen powerful mantras, the book concisely reveals the perfect knowledge of God's proprietorship, control, and the proper utilization of everything in creation for His service. Its importance lies in establishing the personal nature of the Absolute Truth and the necessity of devotional service, providing a crucial entry point for those seeking spiritual understanding beyond material concepts, and setting the stage for deeper philosophical studies in Krishna consciousness.

7) Mukunda-mala-stotra

(by King Kulasekhara, with purports by Srila Prabhupada)

"Mukunda-mala-stotra" by King Kulasekhara, with Srila Prabhupada's purports, is significant for its direct and heartfelt prayers expressing intense devotion, surrender, and longing for Lord Krishna. This collection of verses encapsulates the deep emotions of a pure devotee, offering a timeless example of how to approach the Supreme Lord with humility, love, and earnest supplication. Its importance lies in its ability to inspire genuine spiritual sentiment, serving as a template for personal prayers and fostering a profound sense of connection with the Divine, particularly for those seeking to cultivate pure love of God.

8) Srimad-Bhagavatam

(with purports by Srila Prabhupada)

Srila Prabhupada's multi-volume "Srimad-Bhagavatam" is arguably his magnum opus and the literary embodiment of the Gaudiya Vaishnava tradition, offering an unprecedented and accessible English translation and commentary on this "spotless Purana." Its importance cannot be overstated: it systematically presents the science of God, His various incarnations, His transcendental pastimes, and the highest principles of *bhakti-yoga*, providing a complete spiritual education for humanity. It serves as the primary scripture for millions, guiding them from basic spiritual understanding to the most confidential realizations of pure love for Krishna and the ultimate purpose of life.

9) Sri Chaitanya-Charitamrita

(by Krishnadasa Kaviraja Goswami, with purports by Srila Prabhupada)

"Sri Chaitanya-Charitamrita," with Srila Prabhupada's exhaustive purports, is of paramount importance as the authoritative biography and philosophical exposition of Sri Chaitanya Mahaprabhu, the Golden Avatar and founder of the sankirtana movement. This multi-volume work details Chaitanya Mahaprabhu's life and His profound teachings on the congregational chanting of the Holy Names, the science of Radha-Krishna's loving pastimes, and the highest aspects of *madhurya-rasa*. Its significance lies in providing a complete understanding of the most esoteric and confidential truths of Gaudiya Vaishnavism, establishing the unique contribution of Lord Chaitanya and guiding devotees towards the purest form of love for God

10) Other small and Medium books by Srila Prabhupada

- The Science of Self-Realization

- Teachings of Lord Chaitanya
- Dialectic Spiritualism: A Vedic-philosophic Exposition of the Theistic Philosophy of Bhaktivedanta Swami Prabhupada on the Writings of Western Philosophers
- Readings in Vedic Literature and many more

PHILOSOPHY

"Lord Caitanya's philosophy is that of "inconceivable oneness and difference." This system of philosophy constitutes perfect knowledge of the Absolute Truth."

-Srila Prabhupada Bhagavad Gita as it is 18.78

The central philosophical tenet of Gaudiya Vaishnavism is Achintya Bheda Abheda Tattva, meaning "inconceivable oneness and difference." This doctrine posits that the Supreme Being (Krishna) is simultaneously one with and different from His energies and creations. While He is the ultimate source of everything, He also maintains His distinct personal identity. This resolves the seeming dichotomy between monism and dualism, asserting that both perspectives hold a partial truth. The soul (jiva) is considered an eternal, infinitesimal particle of God, inherently spiritual, and meant for loving service to Him. The material world is a temporary manifestation of God's external energy (maya), designed for the conditioned souls to rectify their desire for independent enjoyment. The ultimate goal is to transcend this material existence and regain one's original spiritual identity as an eternal servant of Krishna, situated in pure love.

a) UPANISHAD

1) Sri Caitanyopanishad

Author: Revealed

- An Upanishad Glorifying Sri Chaitanya: A text that presents Sri Chaitanya Mahaprabhu as the Supreme Personality of Godhead and the embodiment of the teachings of the Upanishads.
- Scriptural Basis for Chaitanya's Divinity: Offers scriptural evidence within the Upanishadic tradition to establish the divine identity of Sri Chaitanya.
- Interpretation of Vedic Texts: Interprets key Vedic passages in light of the teachings and mission of Sri Chaitanya, such as the chanting of the holy names (sankirtana) as the primary religious practice for this age.
- Emphasis on Radha-Krishna Worship: While rooted in Vedic tradition, the text highlights the supreme importance of the worship of Radha and Krishna, the divine couple.

- Guidance on the Path of Bhakti: Provides insights into the principles and practices of bhakti yoga as taught and exemplified by Sri Chaitanya.
- Establishment of Gaudiya Vaishnava Theology: Serves as a foundational scriptural text within the Gaudiya Vaishnava tradition, supporting its unique theological perspectives.
- Revelation of Chaitanya as the Yuga-avatara: Declares Sri Chaitanya as the yuga-avatara, the incarnation of the Supreme Lord for the current age of Kali.

b) GITA COMMENTARIES

These commentaries are not mere academic exercises but deeply devotional expositions, meticulously revealing the supremacy of Radha and Krishna as the ultimate divine couple, the nuanced science of bhakti-yoga, and the intricate flavors of rasa (transcendental mellows). Works like Sanatana Goswami's **Brihad Vaishnava Toshani**, Jiva Goswami's **Krama-sandarbha and Laghu Vaishnava Toshani**, and Visvanatha Chakravarti Thakura's **Sarartha Darshini** form the bedrock of this exegetical tradition, each providing unique insights into the text's philosophy and practical application. Later, figures like Bhaktisiddhanta Sarasvati and A.C. Bhaktivedanta Swami Prabhupada further propagated these Gaudiya perspectives globally, ensuring that the Bhagavatam's message of pure divine love reached every corner, firmly grounding the understanding of this sacred scripture within the specific philosophical framework of Sri Chaitanya Mahaprabhu's teachings.

2) Sarartha varshini Tika on Bhagavad Gita

Author: Vishvanatha Chakravarti Thakur

- Commentary on the Bhagavad Gita: Offers the Gaudiya Vaishnava perspective on the teachings of the Bhagavad Gita.
- Emphasis on Bhakti as the Ultimate Goal: Interprets the Gita through the lens of bhakti yoga as the highest form of spiritual practice.
- Understanding Krishna's Supreme Personality: Highlights the identity of Krishna as the Supreme Personality of Godhead.
- Guidance on Practical Devotion: Connects the philosophical teachings of the Gita with the practical application of devotional principles.
- Harmonization with Gaudiya Theology: Integrates the teachings of the Gita with the broader philosophical framework of Gaudiya Vaishnavism.

3) Śrī Gita Bhūṣaṇa

Author: Baladeva Vidyabhushana

- Consistent Application of Achintya-bhedabheda to Gita Commentary: Unlike some other commentaries that might lean towards specific Vedanta schools,

BaladevaVidyābhūṣaṇa consistently interprets the Bhagavad-gita through the lens of achintya-bhedabheda (inconceivable oneness and difference), providing a unique Gaudiya Vaishnava understanding of its verses.

- Emphasis on Krishna as the Supreme Personality of Godhead Throughout: The commentary firmly establishes and reiterates Krishna's supreme position as the ultimate object of worship and the source of everything, even within the context of the Gita's diverse teachings. This perspective permeates his explanations of various verses.

- Detailed Elaboration on Bhakti-yoga as the Pinnacle of All Yogas: While acknowledging the validity of karma-yoga and jnana-yoga, BaladevaVidyābhūṣaṇa consistently emphasizes bhakti-yoga as the most direct, effective, and ultimately the intended path presented in the Gita for attaining Krishna and spiritual perfection.

- Integration of Gaudiya Vaishnava Theology and Practices: The Gita-bhūṣaṇa seamlessly weaves in specific tenets and practices of Gaudiya Vaishnavism, such as the importance of chanting the holy names, the significance of serving Radha-Krishna, and the role of pure devotional service in achieving the highest goal.

- Clear Refutation of Mayavada Interpretations: Vidyābhūṣaṇa directly addresses and refutes impersonalistic (Mayavada) interpretations of the Gita, firmly establishing the personal nature of the Supreme Lord and the reality of the individual soul's eternal identity and relationship with Krishna.

- Highlighting the Glories of the Lord's Divine Potencies (Shaktis): The commentary often elucidates the role and importance of Krishna's various potencies, particularly

His internal potency (Swarupa Shakti), in understanding His nature and His interactions with the material and spiritual worlds as described in the Gita.

- Emphasis on the Importance of the Spiritual Master and Disciplic Succession: Baladeva Vidyābhūṣaṇa underscores the necessity of receiving the teachings of the Gita through a bona fide spiritual master in a legitimate disciplic succession to grasp its true meaning and avoid misinterpretations.

- Providing Context from Other Relevant Scriptures: While primarily a commentary on the Gita, the Gita-bhūṣaṇa often draws upon other authoritative scriptures like the Srimad-Bhagavatam and the Brahma-saṁhitā to provide a richer and more comprehensive understanding of the Gita's verses from a Gaudiya Vaishnava standpoint.

- Elegant and Scholarly Sanskrit Style: The commentary is written in a refined and scholarly Sanskrit, showcasing BaladevaVidyābhūṣaṇa's deep understanding of grammar, philosophy, and the intricacies of the language, making it a valuable resource for serious students of the Gita.

- A Cornerstone for Gaudiya Vaishnava Understanding of the Gita: The Śrī Gita-bhūṣaṇa stands as the principal and most authoritative commentary on the Bhagavad-gita within the Gaudiya Vaishnava tradition, shaping how its followers understand and interpret this essential scripture in light of their core theological principles.

This commentary concludes the supremacy of Krishna and pure bhakti.

4) Rasika ranjana and Vidvat Ranjan (Commentary on Commentary)

Author: Bhakti Vinoda Thakura

- Śrīla Bhaktivinoda Ṭhākura's first Bengali commentary to the Bhagavad-gītā named 'Rasika-Rañjana' ('That which delights the relishers of rasa') was written in 1886 and was a combined translation/commentary. This commentary was based upon Śrīla Viśvanātha Cakravartī Ṭhākura's Sārārtha-varṣiṇī commentary. The Ṭhākura also gave an elaborate introduction to this work describing the connection between the paths of karma, jñāna and bhakti.
- "Gita Bhaushan", commentary of Srila Baladeva Vidyabhushana on "Srimad Bhagavad Gita" and "Vidvad Ranjan" commentary of Srila Bhakti Vinod Thakura on "Srimad Bhagavad Gita"

5) Bhagavad Gita as it is - Further explained by Srila Prabhupada in lectures

From the mine of Srila Prabhupada's lectures on the Bhagavad Gita, this book is a treasure chest of gems. The Gita verses are followed by lectures Srila Prabhupada gave on those verses.

c) Vedant Sutra Commentary

6) Govinda Bhashya (Commentary on Vedanta Sutra)

Author: Baladeva Vidyabhushana

- The definitive Gaudiya Vaishnava commentary on the Vedanta Sutras.
- Establishes Gaudiya Vaishnavism as a legitimate and distinct school of Vedanta philosophy.
- Systematically refutes the impersonal interpretations (especially Shankara's Advaita Vedanta).
- Philosophically establishes the doctrine of achintya-bhedabheda-tattva (inconceivable simultaneous oneness and difference).
- Solidified the philosophical standing of the Gaudiyasampradaya in debates with other schools.

This commentary was composed following a divine inspiration to address the claim that the Gaudiya Sampradaya lacked a commentary on Vedanta.

d) Srimad Bhagavatam Commentaries/ Compilations

Among the notable Gaudiya Vaishnava commentaries on the Srimad-Bhagavatam are Brihad Vaishnava Toshani by Sanatana Goswami, Laghu Vaishnava Toshani and Krama-sandarbha by Jiva Goswami, Sarartha Darshini by Visvanatha Chakravarti Thakura, Gaudiya Bhashya by Bhaktisiddhanta Sarasvati, and the multi-volume Srimad-Bhagavatam with purports by A.C. Bhaktivedanta Swami Prabhupada.

7) Bhavartha-dipika

Author: Sridhara Swami

- Authoritative Traditional Commentary: A highly respected and widely accepted commentary on the Bhagavata Purana, even predating the Gaudiya school.
- Direct and Lucid Explanations: Offers straightforward and easily understandable explanations of the verses.
- Emphasis on Bhakti Yoga: Clearly establishes the path of bhakti as the primary means of attaining spiritual liberation and divine love.
- Acknowledged by Sri Chaitanya: Sri Chaitanya Mahaprabhu himself expressed appreciation for Sridhara Swami's commentary, indicating its authenticity and value.
- Foundation for Later Commentaries: Serves as a foundational text upon which subsequent Gaudiya Vaishnava commentators built their own interpretations.

8) Sri Brhad-vaisnava-tosani (Tika on Srimad Bhagavatam Canto 10)

Author: Sanatana Goswami

- Commentary on the Tenth Canto: Specifically focuses on providing detailed explanations for the tenth canto of the Srimad Bhagavatam.

- Elaboration on Srimad Bhagavatam: The Srimad Bhagavatam, particularly its Tenth Canto, is central to Gaudiya Vaishnava philosophy as it elaborates on the divine and intimate pastimes of Lord Krishna. Sanatana Goswami's commentary, the Brihad Vaishnava Toshani, delves deeply into these narratives, providing intricate explanations and devotional insights that may not be explicitly stated in the original text or were briefly touched upon by other commentators like Sridhara Svami.

- Devotional Interpretation: It emphasizes the devotional meaning of the verses, contrasting with interpretations that might focus more on impersonal Brahman (brahma-vada). Sanatana Goswami's work is celebrated for its deep devotion and profound understanding of the sweetness of devotion (prema) that Chaitanya Mahaprabhu propagated.

- Understanding Balarama's Rasa-lila: It specifically focuses on certain aspects like Balarama's rasa-lila and his affection for the residents of Vraja (Vrindavan), offering unique insights into these divine relationships.

- Guidance for Devotees: The work also covers aspects of devotional service and the pastimes of divine figures, playing a significant role in understanding the devotional practices central to Vaishnavism.

- Relationship with Laghu Vaishnava Toshani: Sanatana Goswami's nephew, Srila Jiva Goswami, later wrote the Laghu Vaishnava Toshani, which is also a commentary on the Srimad Bhagavatam. Jiva Goswami's commentary is based on Sanatana Goswami's Brihad Vaishnava

Toshani, indicating the foundational importance of Sanatana's work.

9) Laghu-toṣaṇī (Commentary on the Bhagavata Purana)

Author: Jiva Goswami

- Concise yet Profound Commentary: Offers a shorter yet highly insightful commentary on the Bhagavata Purana, focusing on key philosophical and theological points.
- Emphasis on Rasa Theory: Highlights the Gaudiya Vaishnava understanding of rasa (divine mellows) as the ultimate goal of spiritual life.
- Clarification of Difficult Passages: Provides lucid explanations for challenging verses and concepts within the Bhagavata Purana.
- Supporting the Sat Sandarbhas: Often references and complements the philosophical discussions found in Jiva Goswami's Sat Sandarbhas.
- Focus on the Glories of Krishna: Underscores the supreme position and captivating qualities of Lord Krishna as presented in the Bhagavata Purana.

10) SararthaDarshini

Author: VisvanathChakravarti Thakur

- A highly respected and influential commentary on the entire SrimadBhagavatam.
- Provides deep insights into the verses, consistent with Gaudiya Vaishnava siddhanta.
- Elucidates complex philosophical points and narrative details.
- **Emphasizes the rasika (devotional mellow) aspects of the Bhagavatam.**
- Often clarifies the perspectives of previous commentators like Sridhara Swami from a Gaudiya viewpoint.

11) Bhakti-rasāyanam

Author : Śrī Harisūri (also known as Haribābā Śāstrī Paḍhegāonkar)

"Bhakti-rasāyanam" by Śrī Harisūri (composed in the 19th century) is a significant poetic commentary (padyamayī ṭīkā) on the first half of the Tenth Canto of the Śrīmad-Bhāgavatam. Unlike prose commentaries, Harisūri's work presents a verse-by-verse explanation of the main ślokas (verses) from each chapter of the Tenth Canto, utilizing various literary devices like utprekṣā (poetic fancy) and śleṣa (double meaning) to reveal the profound and often hidden devotional meanings within Śrī Kṛṣṇa's pastimes. Revered for its miraculous and insightful interpretations, this unique rasāyanam (a tonic for the heart) aims to pacify heart diseases and nourish pure loving devotion by making the esoteric truths of the Bhāgavatam's Tenth Canto accessible and relishable for the devotee.HG Hari Parshad Prabhu has written a brilliant hindi tretise on this.

12) *Srimad Bhagavata Arka Marichimala (Compilation of key Bhagavatam verses)*

Author: Bhaktivinoda Ṭhākura

- A Carefully Curated Selection of Essential Verses: Bhaktivinoda Thakur meticulously selected verses from the entire Srimad-Bhagavatam that he considered to be the most crucial and illuminating for understanding its core teachings and the path of bhakti-yoga. This compilation acts as a condensed essence of the vast scripture.
- Emphasis on the Supreme Divinity of Lord Krishna: The chosen verses strongly emphasize the supreme position and transcendental nature of Lord Sri Krishna as the Absolute Truth, the source of all existence, and the ultimate object of love and devotion. The compilation systematically establishes Krishna's preeminence.
- Guidance on the Principles and Practice of Bhakti: The Arka-Marichimala highlights verses that delineate the fundamental principles and practical aspects of bhakti, such as the importance of sravanam (hearing), kirtanam (chanting), smaranam (remembrance), and serving the Lord and His devotees. It serves as a concise guide to devotional practice.
- Illumination of Key Philosophical Concepts: The compilation includes verses that elucidate essential philosophical concepts of Gaudiya Vaishnavism, such as

the nature of the soul (jiva), the material world (maya), the relationship between the soul and the Supreme Lord, and the attainment of liberation through divine love.

- A Practical Tool for Study and Meditation: Bhaktivinoda Thakur intended this compilation to be a readily accessible and potent tool for daily study, contemplation, and meditation on the essential teachings of the Srimad-Bhagavatam. It allows devotees to quickly access and reflect upon the most vital verses, deepening their understanding and fostering their spiritual realization.

e) Other philosophical works

13) Vaishnava Siddhanta Mala (Garland of Vaishnava Conclusions)

Author: Bhaktivinoda Ṭhākura

- A Systematic Presentation of Core Vaishnava Principles: This work offers a concise and systematic exposition of the fundamental philosophical and theological conclusions (siddhanta) of the Gaudiya Vaishnava tradition. Bhaktivinoda Thakur presents these key tenets in a clear and organized manner, making them accessible to practitioners and scholars alike.
- Emphasis on the Supreme Authority of Scripture and Tradition: The Siddhanta-mala firmly establishes the

authority of the Srimad-Bhagavatam and other essential Vaishnava scriptures, along with the teachings of the previous acharyas (spiritual teachers) in the disciplic succession. It underscores the importance of scriptural evidence and traditional understanding in comprehending Vaishnava philosophy.

- Clear Articulation of Key Concepts: The work provides lucid explanations of central Vaishnava concepts such as the nature of God (Krishna), the individual soul (jiva), the material world (jagat), the relationship between them (sambandha), the process of devotional service (abhidheya), and the ultimate goal of life (love of God, prayojana).
- A Guide for Proper Understanding and Practice: Vaishnava-siddhanta-mala serves as a practical guide for devotees, ensuring a correct understanding of the philosophical underpinnings of their spiritual practices. By clearly outlining the core principles, it helps practitioners to avoid misconceptions and to cultivate their devotion on a solid foundation of knowledge.
- A Unifying Text for the Gaudiya Vaishnava Sampradaya: Bhaktivinoda Thakur's work has played a significant role in unifying the understanding of Gaudiya Vaishnava philosophy within the sampradaya (tradition). By presenting a clear and authoritative summary of the key conclusions, it helps to maintain doctrinal consistency and promotes a cohesive understanding of the teachings.

14) Brihad Bhagavatamrita (The Great Nectar of the Lord's Devotees)

Author: SanatanaGoswami

Key Points:

- Traces the hierarchy of devotion by following a seeker's journey through different planetary systems and levels of consciousness.
- Establishes the superiority of devotion to Krishna in Vrindavan over all other forms of worship and liberation.
- Analyzes different types of devotees and their relationships with the Lord.
- Reveals the confidential significance of Vrindavan and its inhabitants.
- Culminates in understanding the supreme position of the gopis' love, especially Radharani's.

Śrī Bṛhad-bhāgavatāmṛta, written by SanatanaGoswami and likely completed in the mid-16th century, contains an analysis of the teachings of Chaitanya from an ontological and metaphysical perspective. Its core emphasis includes: narratives exploring the different levels of devotion and the spiritual world; ascertaining the essence of the mercy of the Supreme Lord (Pūrva-khaṇḍa); ascertaining the glories of ŚrīGoloka (Uttar-khaṇḍa); and descriptions of various categories of devotees of Krishna. This scripture thoroughly analyzes the fundamental reality and nature of the divine couple, ŚrīŚrīRādhā-Kṛṣṇa, facilitating their worship.

15) Hari Bhakti Vilasa (The Performance of Devotion to Hari)

Author: Sanatana Goswami (compiled/ elaborated by Gopala Bhatta Goswami)

- Provides the authoritative scriptural codes and conduct for GaudiyaVaishnavas (smriti).
- Details procedures for initiation (diksha), daily practices (ahnika), and deity worship (arcana).
- Outlines observances for festivals like Ekadashi, Janmashtami, etc.
- Gives guidelines for constructing temples and installing deities.
- Explains Vaishnava etiquette, duties of different ashramas, and purification rites.

Śrī Hari-bhakti-vilāsa, authored by SanatanaGoswami and compiled under the guidance of RupaGoswami, sets out guidance for Vaishnava behavior and ritual. Its core teachings provide: detailed instructions on the proper observance of vows and rituals; arrangement of practices for those desiring to obtain krishna-prema (love for Krishna); descriptions of the core aspects of the Vaishnava lifestyle and philosophy; and incorporation of elements from other Vaishnava traditions. This text serves as a comprehensive guide for the daily practices and rituals for those who desire to obtain the ultimate goal of life, krishna-prema.

16) Laghu-bhagavatamrita (A Brief Nectar about the Lord and His Devotees)

Author: Rupa Goswami

- Analyzes the various forms and expansions of the Supreme Lord (Krishna).
- Establishes Krishna as Svayam Bhagavan, the original Supreme Personality of Godhead.
- Categorizes different types of avatars (lila, guna, manvantara, yuga, shaktyavesha).
- Discusses the nature and hierarchy of the Lord's energies.
- Briefly touches upon the prominent devotees of the Lord.

17) Sat Sandarbhas (Six Treatises)

Author: Jiva Goswami

- Provides the comprehensive philosophical foundation (siddhanta) of Gaudiya Vaishnavism.
- Establishes SrimadBhagavatam as the highest scriptural authority (pramana).
- Systematically presents the theology of sambandha (relationship with God), abhidheya (process to attain Him), and prayojana (the ultimate goal - prema).

- Refutes opposing philosophical schools, especially Mayavadaimpersonalism.
- Deeply analyzes the nature of the Absolute Truth, the individual soul, the material world, and divine love.

The Śrī Ṣaṭ-sandarbhas(BhāgavataSandarbha), a collection of six treatises by JivaGoswami, likely completed in the late 16th century, form the philosophical bedrock of Gaudiya Vaishnavism. These works systematically analyze the Śrīmad-Bhāgavatam, emphasizing: Krishna as the Supreme Personality of Godhead (Krishna-sandarbha); the knowledge of the relationship between God, living entities, and the world (sambandha-jñāna) (Tattva, Bhagavat, ParamatmaSandarbhas); the detailed description of bhakti as the means of attaining Krishna (Bhakti-sandarbha); and the analysis of prīti (pure love) as the ultimate goal of life (Priti-sandarbha). This monumental work provides a comprehensive and exhaustive analysis of the essential message of ŚrīmadBhāgavatam, concluding that the highest feature of the Absolute is a personal God.

i) Tattva Sandarbha

Establishes pramana (epistemology), focusing on SrimadBhagavatam.

- Establishes Shabda as the Supreme Pramana (Epistemology): It rigorously argues that the most reliable source of knowledge, especially concerning transcendental realities, is shabda, specifically the Vedic scriptures culminating in the Srimad-Bhagavatam. It differentiates this from other forms of evidence like direct perception and inference, highlighting their limitations in understanding the divine.

- Outlines the Ten Topics of the Srimad-Bhagavatam: It systematically presents the ten fundamental subject matters discussed throughout the Bhagavatam, providing a framework for understanding its comprehensive scope. These topics range from the creation of the universe to the ultimate shelter, Lord Krishna.
- Establishes Krishna as the Supreme Absolute Truth: Through scriptural analysis and logical reasoning, it concludes that Lord Krishna is the ultimate reality, the source of Brahman and Paramatma, and the personal Godhead possessing all transcendental qualities in their fullness.
- Emphasizes the Importance of Disciplic Succession: It highlights the necessity of receiving knowledge through a bona fide spiritual lineage (parampara) to properly understand the profound truths of the scriptures. This ensures the authenticity and correct interpretation of shabda.
- Lays the Foundation for Understanding Gaudiya Vaishnava Theology: This Sandarbha sets the groundwork for the subsequent treatises by establishing the means of knowledge and the ultimate object of that knowledge, thus providing the philosophical basis for the entire Gaudiya Vaishnava worldview.

ii) Bhagavat Sandarbha

Discusses the nature of Bhagavan, establishing Krishna as the source of all incarnations.

- Distinguishes Between Brahman, Paramatma, and Bhagavan: It clearly differentiates the three primary aspects of the Absolute Truth. Brahman is the impersonal, all-pervading aspect; Paramatma is the localized Supersoul; and Bhagavan is the personal Supreme Being, possessing all opulences, and is the ultimate realization.
- Describes the Transcendental Nature of Bhagavan (Krishna): It elaborates on the eternal, blissful, and full-of-knowledge nature of Bhagavan, emphasizing His transcendental body, qualities, and activities, which are beyond the limitations of the material world.
- Explains the Spiritual Realm (Vaikuntha and Goloka): It describes the eternal abodes of the Lord, highlighting the superior nature of GolokaVrindavan as the supreme realm of loving pastimes of Krishna and His most intimate associates.
- Discusses the Lord's Potencies (Shaktis): It outlines the various energies or potencies of Bhagavan, including the internal potency (responsible for the spiritual world and His personal attributes), the marginal potency (the living entities), and the external potency (the material world).
- Establishes Bhagavan as the Source of All Other Realizations: Building on the Tattva-sandarbha, it asserts that Brahman and Paramatma are ultimately emanations or aspects of Bhagavan, thus establishing His supreme position within the Godhead.

iii) Paramatma Sandarbha

Discusses the Supersoul (Paramatma) aspect of the Absolute Truth and the nature of maya.

- Explains the Nature and Function of the Paramatma: It details how the Paramatma, as the localized aspect of the Lord, resides within the hearts of all living beings and pervades the entire universe, acting as the witness and guide.
- Clarifies the Relationship Between the Jiva (Individual Soul) and the Paramatma: It elucidates the intimate connection between the individual soul and the Supersoul, emphasizing that the Paramatma is the constant companion and well-wisher of the jiva, while maintaining their distinct identities.
- Discusses the Lord's Various Incarnations (Avataras): It explains the concept of avataras – the various forms in which the Lord descends into the material world – and clarifies their relationship to the Paramatma and Bhagavan.
- Highlights the Role of the Paramatma in Guiding the Jiva Towards Liberation: It emphasizes that the Paramatma inspires and guides the individual soul towards spiritual realization and liberation from the cycle of birth and death.
- Distinguishes the Paramatma from the Individual Soul: While acknowledging their close relationship, it clearly differentiates the Paramatma, who is infinite and all-knowing, from the finite and conditioned nature of the individual soul.

iv) Krishna Sandarbha

Focuses specifically on Krishna as SvayamBhagavan and His eternal abode, GolokaVrindavan.

- Establishes Krishna as SvayamBhagavan (the Original Personality of Godhead): Through extensive scriptural evidence from the Srimad-Bhagavatam and other Vedic texts, it definitively concludes that Krishna is not merely an avatara but the source of all other incarnations and the ultimate form of Bhagavan.
- Describes Krishna's Eternal Pastimes in GolokaVrindavan: It vividly portrays the transcendental and eternally blissful pastimes of Krishna in His supreme abode, GolokaVrindavan, emphasizing the loving relationships with His intimate associates like the gopis and gopas.
- Establishes the Supreme Position of ShrimatiRadharani: It elucidates the unique and unparalleled position of ShrimatiRadharani as Krishna's most beloved and the embodiment of mahabhava (the highest form of loving emotion), highlighting the central importance of the Radha-Krishna relationship.
- Explains the Concept of Rasa (Divine Sentiment) in Relation to Krishna's Pastimes: It delves into the various rasas or divine emotional exchanges that occur in Krishna's lila, particularly madhurya-rasa (conjugal love), as the most elevated form of spiritual experience.
- Highlights the All-Attractive Nature of Krishna: It emphasizes the inherent attractiveness of Krishna, drawing all living beings towards Him through His beauty, qualities, and pastimes, making Him the ultimate object of love and devotion.

v) Bhakti Sandarbha

Details the theory and practice of bhakti-yoga (abhidheya).

- Establishes Bhakti as the Sole Means to Attain Krishna: It firmly establishes that pure devotional service (bhakti) is the only effective and direct path to realize and attain the Supreme Lord, Krishna, transcending the limitations of karma and jnana (knowledge).
- Explains the Different Stages of Bhakti: It systematically outlines the progressive stages of devotional practice, from initial faith (shraddha) to the development of taste (ruchi), attachment (asakti), and ultimately ecstatic love (bhava and prema).
- Delineates the Nine Processes of Bhakti: It elaborates on the nine primary activities of devotional service: hearing (shravanam), chanting (kirtanam), remembering (smaranam), serving the lotus feet (pada-sevanam), worshiping (archanam), offering prayers (vandanam), acting as a servant (dasyam), considering the Lord one's best friend (sakhyam), and surrendering everything (atma-nivedanam).
- Emphasizes the Importance of Association with Devotees (Sadhu-sanga): It highlights the crucial role of associating with saintly devotees in cultivating and strengthening one's own devotional practice and progressing on the path of bhakti.
- Distinguishes Between Vaidhi Bhakti (Regulated Devotion) and Raganuga Bhakti (Spontaneous Devotion): It explains the two main categories of bhakti, outlining the principles of regulated practice and the more advanced stage of spontaneous loving devotion based on attraction to Krishna's specific pastimes and

associates.

vi) Priti Sandarbha

Analyzes prema-bhakti (divine love) as the ultimate goal (prayojana).

- Describes Priti (Pure Love of God) as the Ultimate Goal of Life: It establishes prema or priti, pure, selfless love for Krishna, as the highest perfection and the ultimate fulfillment of the individual soul's inherent longing.
- Elaborates on the Different Levels and Manifestations of Priti: It explores the various stages and nuances of divine love, including different bhavas (emotional relationships) such as shanta (neutrality), dasya (servitude), sakhya (friendship), vatsalya (parental affection), and madhurya (conjugal love), with madhurya being the highest.
- Highlights the Characteristics of Those Who Have Attained Priti: It describes the ecstatic symptoms and transcendental qualities of devotees who have developed pure love for Krishna, showcasing the transformative power of bhakti.
- Emphasizes the Role of Grace in Attaining Priti: While stressing the importance of devotional practice, it also underscores the crucial role of Krishna's causeless mercy in bestowing the highest levels of prema.
- Concludes the Philosophical Progression of the Sat Sandarbhas: This final treatise represents the culmination of the philosophical journey undertaken in the previous five Sandarbhas, illustrating the ultimate aim of Gaudiya Vaishnava spiritual practice – the

attainment of pure, unalloyed love for Lord Krishna.

18) ŚrīAiśvarya-Kādambinī (The Monsoon of Lord Krishna's Opulence)

Author: BaladevaVidyābhūṣaṇa

- Systematic Exposition of Lord Krishna's Divine Opulences: The primary focus of the Aiśvarya-kādambinī is a comprehensive and systematic presentation of the multifaceted opulences (aiśvarya) of Lord Krishna. Baladeva Vidyābhūṣaṇa meticulously elaborates on Krishna's power, fame, wealth, beauty, knowledge, and renunciation, drawing extensively from scriptural evidence.
- Emphasis on Krishna as the Supreme Personality of Godhead: Building upon the foundational Gaudiya Vaishnava understanding, this work strongly establishes Krishna as the ultimate source of all opulences and the Supreme Personality of Godhead. It refutes any notions of His being subordinate to other deities or impersonal Brahman.
- Integration of Scriptural Evidence from Various Sources: BaladevaVidyābhūṣaṇa draws upon a vast array of Vedic scriptures, including the Srimad-Bhagavatam, Brahma-saṁhitā, and other relevant texts, to support his detailed descriptions of Krishna's glories and opulences. This rich scriptural basis lends significant weight to his arguments.

- Refutation of Mayavada Philosophy: A key aspect of the Aiśvarya-kādambinī is its strong refutation of the Mayavada (impersonalist) philosophy. BaladevaVidyābhūṣaṇa systematically dismantles impersonal interpretations of scripture, firmly establishing the personal nature of the Supreme Truth and the reality of Krishna's transcendental attributes and opulences.
- Inspiring Awe and Reverence for Lord Krishna: By eloquently and thoroughly describing the immeasurable opulences of Lord Krishna, the Aiśvarya-kādambinī aims to inspire deep awe, reverence, and a sense of the Lord's supreme majesty in the hearts of devotees. It cultivates a greater appreciation for His divine grandeur and power.

19)   Śrī   Vedānta-syāmantaka   (The Syamantaka Jewel of Vedanta)

Author: Baladeva Vidyābhūṣaṇa

- A Definitive Gaudiya Vaishnava Commentary on the Brahma Sutras: The Vedānta-syāmantaka serves as the established and authoritative Gaudiya Vaishnava commentary on the Brahma Sutras. This was crucial for the tradition to present its philosophical conclusions within the orthodox framework of Vedanta, demonstrating its scriptural consistency.

- Establishment of Achintya-bhedabheda (Inconceivable Oneness and Difference): The commentary systematically interprets the Brahma Sutras through the lens of the achintya-bhedabheda philosophy, the unique Gaudiya Vaishnava understanding of the relationship between God (Krishna), the individual souls, and the material world. It harmonizes seemingly contradictory scriptural statements by asserting a simultaneous oneness and difference that is beyond human comprehension.
- Refutation of Other Vedantic Schools: BaladevaVidyābhūṣaṇa meticulously refutes the interpretations of other major Vedantic schools, such as Advaita Vedanta (impersonalism), Vishishtadvaita (qualified non-dualism), and Dvaita (dualism), establishing the superiority and scriptural validity of the achintya-bhedabheda perspective.
- Emphasis on Shakti (Potency) and its Role: The Vedānta-syāmantaka gives significant importance to the concept of shakti (divine potency), particularly Krishna's internal potency (Swarupa Shakti) including SrimatiRadharani and the spiritual world. It explains how this potency manifests the diversity within the oneness of the Absolute Truth.
- Foundation for Gaudiya Vaishnava Theology and Practice: By providing a robust Vedantic foundation, this commentary underpins the entire theological and practical system of Gaudiya Vaishnavism. It justifies the worship of Krishna as the Supreme Personality of Godhead, the importance of bhakti (devotional service), and the ultimate goal of attaining love for Radha-Krishna.

20) *Prameya Ratnavali (Jewel Necklace of Truths)*

• 85 •

Author: Baladeva Vidyabhushana

- A concise summary of the core philosophical tenets (prameyas) of Gaudiya Vaishnavism.
- Outlines the nine primary truths as taught by Sri Chaitanya Mahaprabhu.
- Covers topics like the nature of God, the soul, maya, the process of bhakti, and the ultimate goal.
- Serves as a primer for understanding Gaudiyasiddhanta.
- Quotes scriptural evidence to support each point.

ŚrīPrameya-ratnāvalī (A Necklace of Jewels of Philosophical Conclusions) by Baladeva Vidyābhūṣaṇa presents the core philosophical conclusions (prameyas) of Gaudiya Vaishnavism, including: the means of knowing the Supreme Personality of Godhead through the Vedas; the reality of the material world; the difference between jivasand Lord Vishnu; the jivas' nature as servants of God; the different statuses of jivas in conditioned and liberated states; liberation as direct association with Krishna; pure devotional service as the means to liberation; and the three sources of knowledge: direct perception, logic, and Vedic revelation. This book tries to draw a doctrinal connection to Ananda Tirtha (Madhvacharya).

21) Jaiva Dharma (The Constitutional Nature of the Soul)

Author: Bhaktivinoda Ṭhākura

- A novel-like presentation of Gaudiya Vaishnava philosophy through dialogues.
- Explores fundamental questions about the soul's identity, conditioning, and liberation.
- Clearly distinguishes between pure devotion (bhakti) and other paths (karma, jnana, yoga).
- Discusses various philosophical schools and establishes the supremacy of Vaishnavism.
- Covers the entire spectrum from basic principles to advanced concepts like rasa in an accessible narrative format.

Śrī Jaiva-dharma (The Constitutional Religion of the Soul) by Bhaktivinoda Ṭhākura explores: the eternal nature of the soul (jiva); the truth of bodily castes; proper conduct in domestic life; the historical perspective of eternal religion; methods of the soul's release from material bondage; spontaneous devotional service; the truth of the Holy Name; and transcendental rasa. **This philosophical novel presents the superexcellence of the personal theism of the Vaishnavas.**

22) Chaitanya Shikshamrita (The Nectar Teachings of Chaitanya)

Author: Bhaktivinoda Ṭhākura

- A systematic presentation of Sri Chaitanya Mahaprabhu's teachings.
- Analyzes the gradual development of consciousness and spiritual realization.
- Discusses social structure (varnashrama) from a Vaishnava perspective.
- Covers ethical principles, religious duties, and the path of pure devotion.
- Explains the application of Mahaprabhu's teachings in practical life.

23) BhajanaRahasya (The Secrets of Devotional Worship)

Author: Bhaktivinoda Ṭhākura

- A guide to intensive devotional practice (bhajana), particularly chanting.
- Connects verses from Mahaprabhu'sShikshashtakam to different times of the day for meditation.
- Assigns specific sections of the Maha-mantra for meditation based on the ashta kaliya-lila.
- Provides insights into overcoming obstacles in bhajana.
- A manual for deepening one's absorption in the Holy Name and lila.

24) Tattva Sutra (Aphorisms on the Truth)

Author: Bhaktivinoda Ṭhākura

- Presents core Gaudiya Vaishnava philosophy in concise aphorisms (sutras), similar in style to Vedanta Sutra.
- Covers the nature of the Absolute Truth, the soul, maya, and the process of bhakti.
- Provides brief explanations (bhashya) for each sutra.
- A systematic and condensed presentation of siddhanta.
- Demonstrates the logical coherence of Gaudiya Vaishnava philosophy.

25) Śrī Daśa-mūla-tattva (The Ten Foundational Truths)

Author: Bhaktivinoda Ṭhākura

- A Succinct Summary of Core Gaudiya Vaishnava Theology: The Daśa-mūla-tattva presents the ten fundamental philosophical principles of the Gaudiya Vaishnava tradition in a clear and concise format. It acts as a foundational summary, making these essential truths easily understandable and memorable.
- Emphasis on the Supreme Authority of Scripture and Reason: BhaktivinodaṬhākura presents these ten truths

based on both scriptural evidence (primarily the Srimad-Bhagavatam) and sound reasoning, demonstrating the logical coherence and scriptural basis of Gaudiya Vaishnava philosophy.

- Focus on the Nature of God, the Soul, and Their Relationship: The ten truths systematically outline the nature of the Supreme Reality (ŚrīKṛṣṇa), the nature of the individual souls (jīvas), and the eternal and inconceivable (acintya) relationship between them, characterized by both oneness and difference (bhedābheda).
- Establishment of Bhakti as the Supreme Path: The Daśa-mūla-tattva clearly establishes bhakti (pure devotional service to ŚrīKṛṣṇa) as the highest and most effective means to attain spiritual liberation and the ultimate goal of love for God. It underscores the supremacy of devotion over other paths like karma and jñāna.
- A Guiding Framework for Understanding Gaudiya Vaishnavism: This work serves as a vital framework for understanding the core tenets of Gaudiya Vaishnavism. By clearly articulating these ten foundational truths, it provides a solid basis for further study and practice within the tradition, ensuring a consistent and accurate understanding of its philosophical underpinnings.

Śrī Daśa-mūla-tattva (The Ten Foundational Truths) by Bhaktivinoda Ṭhākura outlines the ten fundamental philosophical concepts of Sri Caitanya's teachings: the Vedas as ontological truth; Hari as supreme with all potencies and the ocean of rasa; jivas as His separated manifestations, some devoured by nature and some liberated; everything as both different and non-different from Hari; pure bhakti as the way of attainment; and divine love (prīti) as the objective. These ten pillars contain the whole range of Vedic knowledge.

26) Tattva Viveka (Discerning the Truth)

Author: Bhakti Vinoda Thakur

- A short work comparing and contrasting different philosophical viewpoints (atheism, Buddhism, Advaita, etc.) with Vaishnavism.
- Establishes the rational and scriptural superiority of the Vaishnava conclusion.
- Focuses on discerning eternal truth (tattva) from temporary or partial truths.
- Analyzes the concepts of God, the soul, and the material world.
- A concise apologetic work defending the Vaishnava worldview.

27) Brahmana and Vaishnava

Author: Bhaktisiddhanta Sarasvati Thakur (based on Bhaktivinoda Thakur's ideas)

- Addresses the relationship between caste identity (brahmana by birth) and devotional qualification

(Vaishnava).

- Argues that Vaishnava status, based on devotion, transcends birth-based qualifications.
- Establishes that a pure devotee (Vaishnava) is superior to a brahmana focused only on rituals or birthright.
- Clarifies the true meaning of varnashrama in the context of bhakti.
- A strong statement against casteism within the devotional community.

28) Sarva samvadini

Author: Jiva Goswami

- Comprehensive Philosophy: Presents a broad and deep exposition of Gaudiya Vaishnava philosophy, covering metaphysics, epistemology, and soteriology.
- Harmonization of Scriptures: Systematically reconciles various scriptural statements, including Upanishads, Vedanta-sutra, and the BhagavataPurana.
- Elaboration on Key Concepts: Provides detailed explanations of crucial concepts like jiva (soul), maya (illusion), karma, and bhakti (devotion).
- Refutation of Rival Philosophies: Critically examines and refutes opposing philosophical viewpoints, establishing the supremacy of Vaishnava thought.
- Foundation for the Sandarbhas: Often seen as a companion volume or introduction to JivaGoswami's more extensive Sat Sandarbhas.

29) Dig darshini Tika (Commentary on Hari Bhakti Vilas)

Author: Sanatana Goswami

- Clarification and Elaboration: While Hari-bhakti-vilasa provides the injunctions for devotional practice, the Dig-darshini Tika serves to clarify, elaborate, and provide deeper insights into these rules and their underlying spiritual principles. Sanatana Goswami's commentary often explains the philosophical basis for certain practices, their benefits, and their significance in developing devotion to Lord Krishna.
- Authenticity and Depth: It lends immense authority and depth to the Hari-bhakti-vilasa, ensuring that the prescribed practices are understood not merely as dry rituals but as means to cultivate genuine love for God.
- Addressing Practicalities and Nuances: The Dig-darshini Tika often addresses practical questions and subtle nuances related to the execution of devotional activities, making the Hari-bhakti-vilasa more accessible and practical for devotees.
- Connection to Damodarashtakam: It's also notably connected to the Damodarashtakam, a famous eight-verse prayer to Lord Krishna, where Sanatana Goswami's Dig-darshini Tika provides profound explanations of each verse, revealing deeper meanings of Krishna's pastimes and the emotions of His devotees.

30) Sri Sri Radha Krsna Ganoddesa dipika

Author:Srila Rupa Goswami

This unique work provides a systematic and detailed description of the vast network of eternal associates surrounding Radha and Krishna in their divine pastimes in Vrindavan. It meticulously lists and characterizes their names, forms, qualities, and specific services, a comprehensive depiction rarely found in a single scripture. The book is divided into two main parts: the Brhad-bhaga, which describes associates in vatsalya-rasa (parental affection) and madhurya-rasa (conjugal love), and the Laghu-bhaga, which focuses on those in sakhya-rasa (fraternal friendship) and dasya-rasa (servitude). For advanced practitioners of raganuga-bhakti (spontaneous devotional service), it serves as an essential guide, allowing them to become intimately acquainted with the eternal companions of the Divine Couple and to cultivate an internal meditation on their specific roles and loving services.

31) Vaisnava Etiquette

Author: Sanatana Goswami

- **Daily Conduct (*Sadacara*):** This includes routines for waking, bathing, applying *tilaka*, chanting *mantras*, and performing various devotional acts.

- **Temple Etiquette:** Rules for entering, residing in, and serving in the temple, offering obeisances to the Deity and devotees, and proper behavior during *arati* and other services.
- **Interactions with Devotees:** How to respect and deal with spiritual masters, senior Vaishnavas, equals, and juniors, emphasizing humility and avoiding offenses (*vaisnava-aparadha*).
- **Observance of Vows and Festivals:** Guidelines for fasting on Ekadasi, celebrating Janmashtami, Gaura Purnima, and other Vaishnava festivals.
- **Acceptance of Initiation (*Diksha*) and Shelter:** The qualifications of a genuine spiritual master and disciple, and the importance of proper initiation.

32) Sat Kriya Sara Dipika

Author : Gopala Bhatta Goswami

A comprehensive manual outlining the various *samskaras* (purificatory rites or sacraments) and other essential Vedic rituals to be performed by Vaishnavas throughout their lives. It serves as a practical guide for Vaishnavas to conduct their lives in accordance with *smriti* (religious law) and *grhya-sutra* (household rituals), but specifically adapted and interpreted from a purely Vaishnava perspective. The book details rituals ranging from conception (*garbhadhana*) to death (*antyesti*) and post-death ceremonies, as well as daily observances, rules for deity worship, and various festivals. It essentially provides the framework for a complete Vaishnava *smarta* (traditional Vedic) life, ensuring that all aspects of a devotee's existence are purified and centered on Krishna consciousness. It is a vital text for understanding the practical application of Vaishnava dharma in a traditional setting.

33) Sutra Upasana Vaisnava Puja Vidhi

Author: Srila Rupa Goswami

A concise yet detailed guide for the daily worship of Radha-Krishna Deities within the Gaudiya Vaishnava framework. The term "Sutra Upasana" indicates that it provides the essential principles or "sutras" for worship, focusing on the internal meditation (*dhyana*) and external rituals (*puja*) necessary to properly serve the Divine Couple. It outlines the sequence of offerings, mantras, and meditative practices, beginning with the internal remembrance of Radha and Krishna in their Vrindavan pastimes and then guiding the devotee through the various steps of Deity worship, such as offering *arati*, incense, lamps, and foodstuffs. This text is crucial for *raganuga-bhaktas* who aspire to cultivate an intimate loving relationship with Radha and Krishna through meticulous and heartfelt service, ensuring that their worship adheres to the strict standards set by the Goswamis while fostering deep internal connection.

f) Book on Holy Name

The chanting of the Holy Names of God, particularly the Maha-mantra — "Hare Krishna, Hare Krishna, Krishna Krishna, Hare Hare / Hare Rama, Hare Rama, Rama Rama, Hare Hare" — is considered the most important and effective spiritual practice in Gaudiya Vaishnavism, especially for the current age of Kali. Sri Chaitanya Mahaprabhu extensively propagated this practice, emphasizing that the Holy Name is non-different from Krishna Himself. Chanting cleanses the heart of material desires, purifies the consciousness, and awakens one's dormant love for God. It can be performed individually (japa) on beads or communally (kirtan) with musical instruments and singing. The power of the Holy Name is so potent that it can grant complete spiritual realization, even without strict adherence to other rigorous spiritual disciplines.

1) Harinama Chintamani (The Touchstone of the Holy Name)

Author: Bhaktivinoda Ṭhākura

- A detailed exposition on the science and practice of chanting the Hare Krishna Maha-mantra.
- Presented as a dialogue between Sri Chaitanya Mahaprabhu and Haridasa Thakur.

- Thoroughly discusses the ten offenses (nama-aparadha) to be avoided while chanting.
- Explains the different stages of chanting, from nama-abhasa (shadow) to shuddha-nama (pure name).
- Emphasizes the supreme efficacy and accessibility of the Holy Name in Kali Yuga.

2) Śrī Godruma Kalpāṭavī

Author: Bhaktivinoda Ṭhākura

- Śrī Godruma Kalpāṭavī ("Desire-Tree Grove of Godrumadvīpa") is a collection of Bhaktivinoda Ṭhākura's essays and newsletters from around 1891–1893, focused on the Nāma-haṭṭa (marketplace of the Holy Name) preaching movement in Bengal
- The text draws a vivid analogy between **devotional outreach and a marketplace** where Lord Nityānanda is the chief distributor of the Holy Name, supported by various associates who serve as store-keepers, guards, treasurers, and marketers

<u>Structure of the Nāma-haṭṭa</u>

Bhaktivinoda outlines the roles within this spiritual marketplace:

- **Owner/Dealer:** Lord Nityānanda distributes mercy.

- **Assistants/Traders:** Historical associates like Rūpa, Sanātana, Svarūpa-Dāmodara, Ramananda Rāya, and Advaita Ācārya participate in different spiritual zones vedicyogawisdom.com+1iskconcongregation.com+1.
- **Storekeepers & Treasurers:** Devotees who preserve and distribute the mercy through kīrtana, guidance, and chanting .
- **Guards:** Preserve purity and integrity of the process—Haridāsa Ṭhākura defended the name's glories, others protected its sanctity .

The text is admired for combining strategic organization with devotional fervor; it is "entertaining and emotional, while simultaneously presenting a strategic, scientific, and well-managed method" .

HH Jayapataka Swami's English translation highlights its relevance today for guiding modern devotees in balancing career, family, and preaching

<u>Personalities</u>

"Those who are eternally liberated are always awake to Kṛṣṇa consciousness, and they render transcendental loving service at the feet of Lord Kṛṣṇa. They are to be considered eternal associates of Kṛṣṇa, and they are eternally enjoying the transcendental bliss of serving Kṛṣṇa."

-Srila Prabhupada CC Madhya 22.11

Beyond the Supreme Lord Radha and Krishna, several key personalities are revered in Gaudiya Vaishnavism. Sri Chaitanya Mahaprabhu is the central figure, considered the most merciful incarnation who freely distributed pure love of God. His direct associates, known as the Panca-tattva – Sri Krishna Chaitanya, Prabhu Nityananda, Sri Advaita, Gadadhara, and Srivas – are worshipped collectively. The Six Goswamis of Vrindavan (Rupa, Sanatana, Raghunatha Dasa, Raghunatha Bhatta, Gopal Bhatta, and Jiva Goswami) are foundational for their extensive writings and establishment of the philosophical and devotional framework. Later acharyas (spiritual masters) like Narottama Dasa Thakura, Visvanatha

Chakravarti Thakura, Bhaktivinoda Thakura, and A.C. Bhaktivedanta Swami Prabhupada (the founder of ISKCON) have played crucial roles in preserving and propagating the tradition through the ages.

1) Chaitanya Charitamrita (The Character of the Living Force in Immortality)

Author: Krishna Dasa Kaviraja Goswami

The Chaitanya Charitamrita was composed by Krishnadasa Kaviraja Goswami (c. 1496–1588 CE). He wrote it in his old age in Vrindavan, at the request of the senior devotees there who desired a detailed account of Chaitanya Mahaprabhu's later life and his more esoteric teachings. Although Krishnadasa Kaviraja never personally met Chaitanya Mahaprabhu, he meticulously gathered information from various sources:

- The diaries and notes of intimate associates like Svarupa Damodara Goswami (Chaitanya Mahaprabhu's personal secretary) and Murari Gupta.
- Information from his own guru, Raghunatha Dasa Goswami, who was a direct follower of Chaitanya and served Svarupa Damodara.
- Other early Bengali hagiographies, especially the Chaitanya Bhagavata by Vrindavana Dasa Thakura, which primarily covers Chaitanya Mahaprabhu's earlier life.

Language and Style: The Chaitanya Charitamrita is primarily written in Bengali, but it is interspersed with a vast number of Sanskrit verses. These Sanskrit verses are often quoted from various Vaishnava scriptures (like the Srimad Bhagavatam, Bhagavad-gita, Puranas, and the writings of the Goswamis of Vrindavan) to substantiate and expand upon the points being made. The literary style is rich, poetic, and devotional.

Structure: Like the Chaitanya Bhagavata, it is divided into three main lilas (sections), corresponding to different phases of Chaitanya Mahaprabhu's life:

Adi-lila (Adi = beginning): This section recounts the theological basis of Chaitanya Mahaprabhu's appearance (as the combined form of Radha and Krishna), his early life in Navadvipa, his childhood pastimes as Nimai, his scholarly triumphs, the gathering of his principal associates (Pancha Tattva: Chaitanya, Nityananda, Advaita, Gadadhara, Srivasa), and the initial spread of the sankirtana movement. It lays the philosophical groundwork for understanding his identity.

Madhya-lila (Madhya = middle): This extensive section details Chaitanya Mahaprabhu's life after accepting sannyasa (the renounced order). It covers his travels to South India, his philosophical debates with various scholars (like Sarvabhauma Bhattacharya and Prakashananda Saraswati, where he decisively established the supremacy of bhakti over impersonalism), his regular participation in the Ratha-yatra festival in Puri, and, most importantly, his in-depth instructions to the six Goswamis of Vrindavan (especially Rupa Goswami and Sanatana Goswami) on the science of rasa (transcendental mellows) and devotional service. This section is highly philosophical and theological.

Antya-lila (Antya = final): This concluding section describes Chaitanya Mahaprabhu's later life in Puri, characterized by increasingly intense spiritual ecstasies (maha-bhava) in separation from Krishna (known as vipralambha-bhava). It narrates his daily routines, his intimate interactions with his closest associates, and his Shikshashtakam (eight verses of instruction), which encapsulate the essence of his teachings. This part is filled with profound descriptions of devotional sentiment.

The Śrī Caitanya-caritāmṛta holds immense importance as the primary biography of Sri Caitanya Mahaprabhu and a central theological text. Its core emphasis includes: the life and teachings of Sri Caitanya Mahaprabhu; the understanding of Chaitanya as the combined incarnation of Radha and Krishna; the philosophical concept of Achintya bheda abheda (inconceivable oneness and difference); the importance of chanting the holy names (sankirtana) as the religious practice for the current age (yuga-dharma); and detailed explanations of Gaudiya Vaishnava theology and rasa (devotional sentiments). This text is fundamental to grasping the unique theological contributions of Gaudiya Vaishnavism, particularly the identity of Sri Caitanya Mahaprabhu and the emphasis on sankirtana.

2) Śrī Caitanya-Bhāgavata

Author: VrindavanaDasa Thakura

Original Name and Renaming: Initially, Vrindavana Dasa Thakura's work was known as Chaitanya Mangala. However, because another prominent devotee, Lochana

Dasa Thakura, also wrote a work with the same title, the leading Vaishnava community in Vrindavan decided to rename Vrindavana Dasa's book to Chaitanya Bhagavata to distinguish it.

Structure: The Chaitanya Bhagavata is divided into three main sections (khandas):

Adi-khanda (Beginning Section): This part details the socio-religious conditions of Bengal before Chaitanya Mahaprabhu's advent, his birth in Navadvipa, his childhood pastimes, education, marriage to Lakshmipriya, his scholarly triumphs, his travels, and his eventual acceptance of initiation from Isvara Puri at Gaya. It emphasizes his early life as Nimai Pandita.

Madhya-khanda (Middle Section): This section narrates Chaitanya Mahaprabhu's growing public display of devotion, the gathering of his principal associates (such as Nityananda Prabhu, Advaita Acharya, Srivasa Thakura, Haridasa Thakura, and Gadadhara Prabhu), the inauguration of the sankirtana movement, and significant events like the conversion of the infamous Jagai and Madhai. It concludes with Chaitanya Mahaprabhu accepting the renounced order of sannyasa at the age of 24.

Antya-khanda (Final Section): This part describes Chaitanya Mahaprabhu's life as a sannyasi, his travels, particularly his journey to Puri, his meetings with prominent personalities like Sarvabhauma Bhattacharya, and his interactions with various devotees, exhibiting the highest sentiments of love for Krishna. It also provides detailed accounts of the pastimes of Lord Nityananda.

Likely completed in the mid-16th century, is the earliest full-length biographical work on Sri CaitanyaMahaprabhu. Its core teachings emphasize: the early life and divine nature of Sri Caitanya Mahaprabhu; Chaitanya as an incarnation of Krishna; the significance of chanting the holy names; narratives of Chaitanya's pastimes and interactions with his followers; and the establishment of the Gaudiya Vaishnava tradition. This book provides the foundational narrative of Sri Chaitanya's life and mission, which is essential for understanding the historical and theological underpinnings of Gaudiya Vaishnavism.

3) Śrī Kṛṣṇa Caitanya Caritra Mahākāvyam

Author: Murāri Gupta

By Murāri Gupta is an epic poem chronicling the life and mission of Sri Caitanya, describing His ecstatic moods and divine nature. This work is considered an important source for Sri Caitanya's **early life.**

4) Śrī Caitanya Mahāprabhu: His Life and Precepts

Author: Bhaktivinoda Ṭhākura

- **A Modern Synthesis of Historical Narrative and Philosophical Essence:** BhaktivinodaṬhākura masterfully blends a concise historical account of Sri Chaitanya Mahaprabhu's life with a clear and accessible presentation of His core teachings and the underlying Gaudiya Vaishnava philosophy. It bridges the biographical and the doctrinal in a way that is both informative and inspiring for a contemporary audience.

- **Emphasis on the Universal and Rational Aspects of Chaitanya's Teachings:** While deeply rooted in tradition, BhaktivinodaṬhākura highlights the universal and rational aspects of Sri Chaitanya's precepts, presenting them in a way that resonates with modern thought and emphasizes the inherent logic and scientific basis of spiritual inquiry as understood within Gaudiya Vaishnavism.

- **Contextualization of Chaitanya's Movement within Indian Religious History:** The book provides a valuable historical context for Sri Chaitanya's appearance and the Gaudiya Vaishnava movement, situating it within the broader landscape of Indian religious and philosophical traditions, while also asserting its unique contributions and supreme position.

- **Clear Articulation of the Core Philosophical Tenets:** BhaktivinodaṬhākura succinctly outlines the key philosophical principles of Gaudiya Vaishnavism as taught by Sri Chaitanya, including the nature of God (Krishna), the soul, the material world, and the path of bhakti (devotional service). He presents these complex ideas in a lucid and easily understandable manner.

- **A Call for Practical Application and Spiritual Transformation:** Beyond mere intellectual understanding, the book serves as an inspiring call for the practical application of Sri Chaitanya's teachings in one's own life. It emphasizes the transformative power of nama-sankirtana (the congregational chanting of the holy names) and sincere devotion in achieving spiritual awakening and the ultimate goal of love for God.

5) Commentaries on Chaitanya Charitamrita&Bhagavatam

Author: Bhaktisiddhanta Sarasvati Thakur (Anubhashya on CC, Gaudiya Bhashya on Bhagavatam)

- Provide deep philosophical insights consistent with the teachings of Bhaktivinoda Thakur.
- Strongly emphasize the importance of guru and parampara.
- Forcefully refute Mayavadaimpersonalism and various deviations (apasampradayas).
- Stress the practical application of teachings and the importance of preaching.
- Highlight the divinity of Sri Chaitanya Mahaprabhu and the purity of the Holy Name.

6) Chaitanya Mangala

Author: Lochana Dasa Thakura

- **Early Biography** of Sri Chaitanya: One of the earliest and most influential biographies of Sri Chaitanya Mahaprabhu.
- Focus on Chaitanya's Early Life and Activities: Details the childhood, youth, and early preaching of Sri

Chaitanya.

Structure: The Chaitanya Mangala is typically divided into four sections:

- **Sutra Khanda:** A prelude that sets the stage for Lord Chaitanya's appearance.
- **Adi Khanda:** Covers Chaitanya Mahaprabhu's early life up to his trip to Gaya.
- **Madhya Khanda:** Describes events in Mahaprabhu's later life, including his meeting with Sarvabhauma Bhattacharya.
- **Shesh Khanda:** The final section, focusing on his remaining pastimes.
- **Poetic and Devotional:** Lochana Dasa Thakura's "Chaitanya Mangala" is particularly cherished for its poetic beauty and profound devotional sentiment. It's often described as a rasatmaka-sastra (a book full of rasa or transcendental mellows), emphasizing the emotional depth of Chaitanya Mahaprabhu's pastimes.
- **Unique Details:** It sometimes contains details and conversations not found in the other major biographies, such as intimate exchanges between Lord Chaitanya, His mother Saci Devi, and His wife Vishnupriya Devi, especially concerning His acceptance of sannyasa (renunciation).
- **Influenced by Murari Gupta:** Lochana Dasa Thakura drew heavily from the Sanskrit Sri Krishna-Chaitanya-Charitamritam by Murari Gupta, an early biographer of Chaitanya Mahaprabhu.

7) Gaura Ganoddesha Dipika (Identities of Chaitanya's associates)

Author: Kavi Karnapura

- **Revealing the Eternal Identities of Chaitanya's Followers:** The primary purpose of the Gaura-ganoddesha-dipika is to identify the eternal spiritual identities of the principal associates of Sri Chaitanya Mahaprabhu within the pastimes of Radha and Krishna in Vrindavan. It establishes direct connections between the gopis and gopas of Krishna's lila and the devotees who appeared with Chaitanya Mahaprabhu.

- **Establishing the Theologically Significant Concept of Gaura-lila as a Manifestation of Krishna-lila:** The work underscores the Gaudiya Vaishnava theological understanding that the pastimes of Sri Chaitanya Mahaprabhu (Gaura-lila) are a direct manifestation and continuation of the pastimes of Radha and Krishna (Krishna-lila). By revealing the previous identities of Chaitanya's associates, it reinforces this central tenet.

- **Providing Essential Information for Understanding Gaudiya Vaishnava Lineage and Succession:** The Dipika serves as a foundational text for understanding the lineage (parampara) and the roles of key figures in the Gaudiya Vaishnava tradition. Knowing the eternal identities of the early devotees helps to contextualize their contributions and their significance in the disciplic succession.

- **Deepening Devotional Understanding and Appreciation:** By understanding the intimate connections between Chaitanya's associates and the eternal residents of Vrindavan, devotees can cultivate a deeper and more profound appreciation for their roles and contributions to the Gaura-lila. This knowledge enhances one's devotional understanding and fosters greater reverence for these exalted personalities.

- **A Key Reference Work for Gaudiya Vaishnava Scholarship:** The Gaura-ganoddesha-dipika remains an indispensable reference work for scholars and practitioners of Gaudiya Vaishnavism. It provides crucial insights into the theological framework of the tradition and serves as the authoritative source for understanding the spiritual identities of Chaitanya Mahaprabhu's inner circle.

8) Bhakti Ratnakar

Author: Narahari Cakravarti Thakura

- **Lives of Devotees:** It primarily describes the lives and activities of prominent devotees who followed Sri Chaitanya Mahaprabhu, especially after His disappearance.
- **Propagation of Bhakti:** It illuminates how leading devotees, particularly figures like Srinivasa Acarya and Narottama Dasa Thakura, endeavored to spread the Lord's teachings, especially in Bengal.
- **Historical Context:** The book provides a vivid historical account of the mood and events within the Vaishnava community after Chaitanya Mahaprabhu's manifest

pastimes concluded.

- **Glorification of Holy Places:** It includes descriptions and glorification of various holy places, particularly in Vrindavana and Navadvipa, connecting them to the pastimes of the Lord and His associates.

- **Inspiration and Reassurance:** It highlights how devotees faced with loss and challenges found inspiration and reassurance from the remaining associates and through divine interventions (like dreams), emphasizing the Lord's desire for His message to be distributed.

- **Emphasis on Humility:** The author, Narahari Cakravarti, exemplifies and emphasizes humility as a core devotional quality, often describing himself as a "worthless person" in alignment with Chaitanya Mahaprabhu's teachings on humility.

- **Compilation of Pastimes:** It is a valuable compilation of fascinating pastimes of various devotees, including Sri Jahnava-devi, Viracandra Prabhu, and Gopala Bhatta Gosvami.

- **Theological and Philosophical Significance:** While detailing historical narratives, the book also carries significant theological and philosophical weight, reinforcing the doctrines of the Bhakti cult.

9) Namacarya: The Life of Srila Haridasa Thakura

Author: Rupa-vilasa Dasa.

A comprehensive and accessible biography of Haridasa Thakura, the revered Namacharya (preceptor of the Holy Name) in the Gaudiya Vaishnava tradition. Drawing from various historical and scriptural sources, the book meticulously narrates the extraordinary life of this fearless devotee, from his birth in a Muslim family to his unwavering dedication to chanting the Holy Names despite intense persecution. It vividly portrays his profound humility, spiritual power, and his central role as an intimate associate of Sri Chaitanya Mahaprabhu, ultimately serving as an inspiring testament to the transformative potency of pure devotion and the Holy Name.

10) Sri Nityananda Caritamrta

Author: Srila Vrindavan Dasa Thakura

The essence of Lord Nityananda Prabhu's divine pastimes. His boundless love as he fearlessly reaches out to all, transcending social barriers and offering solace to weary hearts. His divine grace is an invitation to embrace the eternal dance of divine love.

The transformative power of Lord Nityananda Prabhu's mercy—a boundless ocean that awakens dormant love for Krishna within us.

11) Narottama Vilasa

Author : Narahari Cakravarti Thakura

a crucial biographical account detailing the life and missionary activities of the revered Gaudiya Vaishnava saint Narottama Dasa Thakura, particularly focusing on his efforts to establish the pure teachings of Chaitanya Mahaprabhu in Bengal after returning from Vrindavana with the Goswamis' scriptures.

12) Srila Bhaktivinoda Thakura: His Life and Works

Author : Srila Bhaktisiddhanta Sarasvati

"Srila Bhaktivinoda Thakura: His Life and Works," primarily compiled by his son Srila Bhaktisiddhanta Sarasvati, provides an in-depth biography of this pioneering acharya who intellectually and practically revitalized Gaudiya Vaishnavism in the late 19th century, laying the groundwork for its global spread.

13) Bābājī Mahārāja: Two Beyond Duality: Biographies of Their Divine Graces

Author: Rupa vilasa Dasa

"Bābājī Mahārāja: Two Beyond Duality," a more recent compilation by Rupa-vilasa Dasa, offers dedicated biographical insights into the lives of the highly renounced and spiritually powerful saints, Srila Jagannatha Dasa Babaji and Srila Gaura Kisora Dasa Babaji, illuminating their austerity and profound spiritual realization.

14) Śrī Bhaktisiddhānta Vaibhava

Author: Bhakti Vikasa Swami

"Śrī Bhaktisiddhānta Vaibhava" by Bhakti Vikasa Swami is the definitive, multi-volume biography of Srila Bhaktisiddhanta Sarasvati Goswami Prabhupada, chronicling his monumental mission to establish the Gaudiya Math and fearlessly combat philosophical deviations, thus preserving the purity of the Vaishnava tradition.

15) Srila Prabhupada-lilamrta

Author: Satsvarupa Dasa Goswami

"Srila Prabhupada-lilamrta" by Satsvarupa Dasa Goswami serves as the authorized, extensive biography of A.C. Bhaktivedanta Swami Prabhupada, documenting his incredible journey from a humble renunciate to the spiritual master who successfully brought Krishna consciousness to the entire world by establishing ISKCON.

Prayers

"Narottama dāsa Ṭhākura's versions are accepted as Vedic versions, śruti-pramāṇa. Viśvanātha Cakravartī Ṭhākura says that the statements of Narottama dāsa Ṭhākura are as good as Vedic evidences. Therefore we quote from Narottama dāsa Ṭhākura often."

-Srila Prabhupada Vrndavana, November 13, 1972

Gaudiya Vaishnava prayers are deeply rooted in expressing surrender, devotion, and longing for divine service. While the chanting of the Holy Name is paramount, various other prayers and stotras (hymns) are offered. These often express humility, a recognition of one's fallen state, and an ardent desire for Krishna's mercy and to engage in His service. Many prayers are compositions of the Goswamis and later acharyas, such as Rupa Goswami's Stava-mala and Raghunatha Dasa Goswami's Vilapa Kusumanjali. The Bhagavatam itself contains numerous prayers offered by great devotees. The mood of vipralambha-bhava (love in separation) is a prominent theme, where devotees express intense yearning for the

Lord's presence and service, similar to the mood of Radha and the gopis.

1) Prema Bhakti Chandrika (Moonlight Rays of Loving Devotion)

Author: Narottam Das Thakur

- **Focus on Raganuga Bhakti and Manjari Bhava:** While Prarthana emphasizes the mood of humility and longing for mercy, Prema Bhakti Chandrika goes deeper into the nuances of raganuga-bhakti (spontaneous devotional service) and manjari-bhava (the mood of a maidservant of Srimati Radharani). It outlines the process of developing intense attachment to Krishna, specifically in the mood of the eternal residents of Vrindavan.
- **Practical Guidance for Internal Meditation:** It provides practical guidance for internal meditation on one's spiritual form (siddha-deha) and aspiring to participate in the eternal pastimes (lila) of Radha and Krishna in Vrindavan, particularly in the role of a manjari (confidential maidservant of Radharani).
- **Description of Prema and its Development:** The songs explain the nature of prema (pure love of God) and how it gradually develops through the stages of sadhana-bhakti (devotional practice) and bhava-bhakti (the awakening of transcendental emotions).
- **Glorification of Vrindavan and its Residents:** The text deeply glorifies the sacred land of Vrindavan and the intimate, loving relationships of its eternal residents

with Radha and Krishna.

- **Sri Guru Carana Padma Kevala Bhakati Sadma**: This is a very common Guru-vandana (prayer to the spiritual master) and is frequently sung during Guru Puja (worship of the spiritual master).

2) Prarthana (Prayers)

Author: Narottam Das Thakur

- A collection of deeply moving devotional songs expressing humility and intense prayer.
- Often laments the fallen condition and begs for causeless mercy.
- Glorifies Sri Chaitanya, Nityananda Prabhu, Advaita Acharya, and the Goswamis.
- Prays for purification, attachment to Vrindavan, and service in madhurya-rasa.

Practical Guide to Bhakti: Prarthana serves as a practical guide for aspiring devotees on how to cultivate the mood of humility, surrender, and intense longing for Krishna.

- Heart of Bhakti: It is considered one of the three essential books that Srila Bhaktisiddhanta Sarasvati Thakura (the spiritual master of Srila Prabhupada) recommended for his disciples to know, practice, and realize for attaining the perfection of life, along with Prema-bhakti-candrika and Upadesamrita.

- Widely sung by Gaudiya Vaishnavas, encapsulating the mood of devotion.
- **TYPES OF PRAYERS**

1. Prayers of Humility and Self-Reproach: Dainya-bodhika (or Svadhainyabodhika)
2. Prayers for Mercy and Shelter: Samprarthanatmika (or Vijnapti)
3. Prayers Glorifying the Guru and Vaishnavas: Vaiṣṇava-mahimā-prakāśikā (or Guru-Vaiṣṇava-vijnapti-rupa)
4. Prayers Expressing Longing and Aspiration: Lālasāmayī (or Svābhiṣṭa-lālasā)
5. Prayers of Lamentation due to Separation: Vilapātmikā (or Viraha-janita-vilāpa)
6. Prayers Affirming Loyalty and Dependence: Niṣṭhā-dyotikā (or Sva-niṣṭhā)

3) Saranagati (Surrender)

Author: Bhaktivinoda Ṭhākura

- A collection of devotional songs expressing the six limbs of surrender (shat-angasaranagati).
- The six limbs are: accepting favorable, rejecting unfavorable, faith in Krishna's protection, accepting Krishna as maintainer, humility, and full self-surrender.
- Six Limbs of Surrender: The Sharanagati book is structured around the six limbs (anga) of surrender,

which were originally enumerated by Srila Rupa Goswami in his Bhakti-rasamrita-sindhu. Bhaktivinoda Thakura beautifully elaborates on each of these limbs through his Bengali songs (bhajans):

- **Ānukūlyasya Saṅkalpa (Accepting what is favorable for devotion)**: The determination to wholeheartedly accept all activities and circumstances that are conducive to one's spiritual advancement and the satisfaction of Krishna.

- **Prātikūlyasya Varjanam (Rejecting what is unfavorable for devotion)**: The resolute determination to give up all actions, thoughts, and associations that are detrimental to one's devotional life or displease Krishna.

- **Rakṣiṣyatīti Viśvāsaḥ (Firm faith that Krishna will protect)**: Unwavering conviction and trust that Lord Krishna is one's sole maintainer and protector in all circumstances, both material and spiritual. This faith alleviates anxiety and fear.

- **Goptṛtve Varaṇam (Accepting Krishna as one's sole maintainer/guardian)**: Consciously choosing Krishna as one's only shelter and provider, recognizing that He is the ultimate sustainer of all beings.

- **Ātma-nikṣepaḥ (Self-dedication or full surrender of oneself)**: The complete offering of one's body, mind, words, and ego to the service of Krishna, giving up all sense of proprietorship.

- **Kārpaṇya (Humility)**: A deep sense of humility, recognizing one's own insignificance, helplessness, and fallen nature, and feeling a profound dependence on the Lord's mercy.

4) Gita mala (A Garland of Songs)

Author: Bhaktivinoda Ṭhākura

- Another collection of devotional Bengali songs.
- Covers a wide range of topics including glorification of the Holy Name, Vaishnava etiquette, personal struggles, and philosophical points.
- Contains narratives and teachings in simple, poetic language.
- Includes famous songs describing the "marketplace of the Holy Name" (nama-hatta).
- Aimed at instructing and inspiring devotees through accessible songs.

5)Gitavali (Song collection)

Author: Bhaktivinoda Ṭhākura

- Expression of Deep Yearning and Devotional Emotions: Gitavali is a heartfelt outpouring of Bhaktivinoda Thakur's profound longing and various devotional emotions (bhavas) for Radha and Krishna. The songs articulate a wide spectrum of feelings, from intense separation and humility to joyful anticipation and ecstatic love for the Divine Couple.
- Guidance on the Stages of Bhakti: The collection often reflects the progressive stages of bhakti (devotional

service), guiding the practitioner through initial surrender, purification, cultivation of good qualities, and the eventual attainment of pure love. The songs serve as a roadmap for spiritual advancement.

- Emphasis on Nama-Sankirtana and the Holy Name: Many songs in Gitavali underscore the paramount importance of nama-sankirtana (the congregational chanting of the holy names of God) as the primary spiritual practice for this age. Bhaktivinoda Thakur passionately advocates for the power and efficacy of the Hare Krishna maha-mantra.

- Didactic and Instructive in Nature: While deeply emotional, the songs in Gitavali also carry a strong didactic element. They often impart essential Vaishnava teachings, philosophical truths, and practical instructions on how to live a life dedicated to Krishna consciousness.

- A Blend of Bengali and Sanskrit: Gitavali features songs composed in both Bengali and Sanskrit, reflecting Bhaktivinoda Thakur's mastery of both languages and his desire to reach a wider audience with his devotional message. The combination adds a rich and diverse texture to the collection.

6)KalyanaKalpataru (The Desire Tree of Auspiciousness - Songs)

Author: Bhaktivinoda Ṭhākura

- Kalyana Kalpataru (1880) by Srila Bhaktivinoda Thakura is a revered Bengali devotional songbook in the Gaudiya Vaishnava tradition. Structured as a symbolic "wish-fulfilling tree," it comprises 62 songs divided into three thematic branches, guiding devotees from spiritual instruction to deep emotional devotion.
- A Prayer for Spiritual Welfare and Auspiciousness: The title itself, "The Desire Tree of Auspiciousness," indicates the central theme. The songs in Kalyana-kalpataru are essentially prayers and heartfelt appeals to the Lord for spiritual well-being, the removal of obstacles, and the bestowal of divine grace and auspiciousness in the devotee's life.
- Systematic Progression Through Devotional Practices: The collection is often structured to guide the reader through various essential aspects of devotional life. It covers topics such as the importance of the spiritual master, the need for detachment from material pursuits, the cultivation of humility and tolerance, and the earnest practice of chanting the holy names.
- **Upadeśa (Spiritual Advice)**

This branch offers 19 songs addressing common spiritual pitfalls, such as lust, pride, and attachment to material pleasures. Bhaktivinoda provides guidance to help devotees overcome these obstacles and cultivate a sincere devotional life.

- **Upalabdhi (Attainment of Realization)**

Comprising 14 songs, this section delves into the internal transformations a devotee experiences, including:

Anutāpa (Repentance)
Nirveda (Detachment from material desires)
Sambandha-Abhidheya-Prayojana (Understanding one's relationship with Krishna, the means to attain Him, and the ultimate goal)

- **Ucchvāsa (Overflowing Spiritual Emotions)**

This final branch contains 29 songs expressing deep devotional sentiments, such as:
Prārthanā Dainya-mayi (Prayers of humility)
Prārthanā Lālasa-mayi (Prayers of longing)
Vijñapti (Confidential confessions)
Ucchvāsa Kīrtana (Chanting of the Lord's names, forms, qualities, pastimes, and divine mellows)
Bhaktivinoda Thakura composed Kalyana Kalpataru to guide souls entangled in material existence towards the path of pure devotion. He envisioned the songs as a means to awaken spiritual consciousness, offering solace and direction to those seeking a deeper connection with the Divine. The work is esteemed for its clarity, depth, and heartfelt expression, making it a cherished resource for practitioners of bhakti-yoga.

7) Stava mala

Author: Rupa Goswami

- Garland of Prayers: A collection of heartfelt prayers and hymns offered to various deities and aspects of the divine.

- Expression of Deep Devotional Feelings: Reveals the profound love, longing, and surrender of a pure devotee.
- Insight into Gaudiya Theology: Subtly incorporates key theological principles within the devotional expressions.
- Model for Devotional Prayer: Serves as an example of how to approach the divine with sincerity and devotion.
- Focus on Radha-Krishna: Many of the prayers center on the divine couple, Radha and Krishna, and their eternal pastimes.

8) Stavavali (Collection of Prayers)

Author: Raghunatha Dasa Goswami

- A collection of intensely personal and devotional prayers, hymns, and poems.
- Expresses deep longing (vipralambha) for the service of Radha and Krishna.
- Reveals the mood of a manjari (Radharani's confidential maidservant).
- Emphasizes humility, renunciation, and desperate hankering for divine grace.
- Includes famous works like VilapaKusumanjali and ManahShiksha.

9) Padyavali

Author: Rupa Goswami

- Anthology of Devotional Verses: A collection of devotional poems and verses from various sources, including RupaGoswami himself and other devotees.
- Variety of Devotional Expressions: Showcases a wide range of emotions, moods, and perspectives within devotional service.
- Preservation of Important Vaishnava Poetry: Serves as a valuable compilation of significant verses from the Gaudiya tradition and beyond.
- Source of Inspiration and Guidance: Provides devotees with poetic expressions of devotion that can inspire their own spiritual practice.
- Insight into the Devotional Landscape: Offers a glimpse into the rich literary and devotional culture of the Vaishnava tradition.

10) Stavamrita Lahiri

Author: Visvanath Chakravarti Thakur

- **Collection of Devotional Hymns:** "Stavamrita Lahiri" is a comprehensive collection comprising 28 small devotional works, hymns, and prayers.
- **Author and Purpose:** It was composed by Visvanatha Cakravarti Thakura, a prominent Vaishnava acharya, with the purpose of glorifying various deities, gurus,

and sacred places.

- **Focus on Bhakti and Guru-Parampara:** The work emphasizes the path of *bhakti* (devotion) and often includes prayers and glorifications of the guru lineage (*guru-parampara*), detailing the spiritual succession.
- **Descriptions of Deities and Pastimes:** It contains verses that describe the forms, qualities, and pastimes of various deities, particularly Radha and Krishna, and their associates.
- **Meditative and Instructive:** The hymns are intended to aid devotees in their meditation and spiritual practices, providing insights into devotional sentiments and the glories of the divine.
- **Gurvashtakam (Eight Prayers Glorifying the Spiritual Master)** Given in Stavamrita Lahiri.Eight verses describing the qualities and activities of a bona fide spiritual master.Emphasizes the guru's role in connecting the disciple to Krishna.Highlights the guru engaging disciples in various services, especially temple worship and kirtan.Stresses that the guru represents Krishna's mercy.**Sung daily in ISKCON Temples worldwide.**

PLACES SPIRITUAL

"Vrajabhūmi" refers to Mathurā-Vṛndāvana, and Gauḍa-maṇḍala-bhūmi includes Navadvīpa. Therefore, anyone living in Navadvīpa-dhāma, knowing Kṛṣṇa and Śrī Caitanya Mahāprabhu to be the same The Lord has made it convenient for the conditioned soul to live in Mathurā, Vṛndāvana and Navadvīpa"

-Srila Prabhupada ŚB 10.1.28

The spiritual heartland of Gaudiya Vaishnavism is Vrindavan, a town in Uttar Pradesh, India, where Krishna performed many of His earthly pastimes. Other significant holy places include Mayapur in West Bengal, the birthplace of Sri Chaitanya Mahaprabhu, and Jagannath Puri in Odisha, where Chaitanya Mahaprabhu resided for many years and where the famous Jagannath Temple stands. These places are considered sacred because they are eternally connected to the divine pastimes of Radha and Krishna and Sri Chaitanya Mahaprabhu. Pilgrimage to these sites is highly encouraged as it purifies the heart, deepens faith, and offers the opportunity to connect with the divine energies present there. Devotees often engage in parikrama (circumambulation) of these holy places, visiting various temples and sites associated with the Lord's pastimes.

<u>VRINDAVAN</u>

1) GovindaVrindavanastakam

Author: RupaGoswami

- Eight Verses on Govinda in Vrindavan: A short and beautiful poem describing the enchanting form and activities of Lord Govinda in the sacred land of Vrindavan.
- Focus on Krishna's Beauty and Charm: Highlights the captivating aspects of Krishna's appearance and demeanor.
- Evocation of Vrindavan's Atmosphere: Creates a vivid picture of the idyllic and spiritually charged environment of Vrindavan.
- Expression of Devotional Yearning: Conveys the devotee's deep longing to serve Govinda in Vrindavan.
- Concentrated Essence of Vrindavan rasa: Captures the sweet and intimate loving exchanges that occur in Krishna's abode.

2) Vraja-riti-chintamani

Author: Vishvanatha Chakravarti Thakur

- Thoughts on the Practices of Vraja: Explores the specific customs, traditions, and daily life within the sacred land of Vrindavan.
- Understanding the Mood of Vrindavan: Aims to help devotees understand and cultivate the unique devotional atmosphere of Krishna's abode.
- Guidance on Internalizing Vrindavan Consciousness: Provides insights into how to live and practice devotion with the spirit of a resident of Vraja.
- Emphasis on Spontaneous Devotion (raga-marga): Likely touches upon the principles of raga-marga bhakti, the path of spontaneous loving devotion.
- Practical Application of Vraja Philosophy: Connects the philosophical understanding of Vrindavan with practical devotional life.

3) Mathura Mahatmya

Author: Rupa Goswami

- Glories of Mathura: Details the spiritual significance and transcendental importance of Mathura, Krishna's birthplace.
- Description of Sacred Sites: Enumerates and glorifies the various holy places and forests within the Mathura region.
- Emphasis on the Benefits of Pilgrimage: Highlights the spiritual merits attained by visiting and residing in Mathura.

- Connection to Krishna's Pastimes: Explains the intimate connection of Mathura to Krishna's childhood and early life.
- Inspiring Veneration for the Holy Land: Aims to cultivate deep respect and reverence for the sacred geography of Krishna's lila.

4) Mathura Mandala Parikrama

Author: Bhaktivinoda Ṭhākura

1. **Guide to the Holy Land of Mathura and Vraja:** This book functions as a spiritual travelogue and guide for performing *parikrama* (circumambulation) of the broader Mathura region, which includes Vrindavana and the twelve forests of Vraja.
2. **Detailed Descriptions of Sacred Sites:** Bhaktivinoda Thakura meticulously describes the various holy places within Mathura Mandala, providing their scriptural references, historical significance, and the specific pastimes (*lilas*) of Krishna and Balarama that occurred there.
3. **Connecting Places to Krishna's Lila:** The central purpose is to immerse the reader in the understanding that every inch of Mathura Mandala is imbued with Krishna's divine presence and holds the memory of His enchanting pastimes.
4. **Aids for Pilgrims and Meditators:** It's an invaluable resource for pilgrims physically undertaking the *parikrama* and equally for those who perform mental

parikrama (*manasi-seva*), helping them visualize and meditate on Krishna's *lilas* in their original settings.

5. **Cultivation of Vraja-bhava:** Through detailed geographical and spiritual descriptions, the book aims to help the devotee cultivate a deep attachment and spiritual mood (*bhava*) for Vraja-bhumi, the land of Krishna's eternal pastimes.

5) Sri Vrindavana Mahimanrta

Author: Prabodhananda Sarasvati

1. **Exaltation of Vrindavana Dham:** "Sri Vrindavana Mahimanrta" ("The Nectar of Vrindavana's Glories") is a poetic and highly devotional work that exclusively glorifies the transcendental land of Vrindavana, the eternal abode of Radha and Krishna.
2. **Profound Spiritual Realizations:** The author, Prabodhananda Sarasvati, a direct contemporary and associate of Sri Chaitanya Mahaprabhu, pours out his profound spiritual realizations and ecstatic experiences of Vrindavana, describing its every detail as surcharged with divine bliss.
3. **Emphasis on the Sweetness of Vrindavana:** The book paints a vivid picture of Vrindavana's unparalleled beauty, its trees, rivers, birds, and animals, all seen as participants in the intimate *lilas* of the Divine Couple, imbued with the highest sweetness (*madhurya*).
4. **Inspiring Attachment to the Dham:** It aims to inspire an intense and unwavering attachment (*dham-priti*) to

Vrindavana Dham, convincing the reader that living in or meditating upon Vrindavana is the highest form of spiritual practice.

5. **Guide for Raganuga-bhakti and Lila-Smaranam:** For those aspiring to *raganuga-bhakti*, this text is crucial as it details the spiritual atmosphere and specific locations of Krishna's confidential *lilas*, aiding in internal meditation (*lila-smaranam*) and ultimately helping one develop a mood of service to Radha-Krishna in Vrindavana.

<u>NAVADVIPA</u>

6) Sri Navadvipa Dhama Mahatmya (Glorification of Navadvipa)

Author: Bhaktivinoda Ṭhākura

- Establishing Navadvipa as the Supreme Holy Land: The Mahatmya emphatically establishes Sri Navadvipa-dhama as the most sacred and supremely auspicious place in the entire spiritual universe. It reveals Navadvipa as non-different from Vrindavan and the heart of all holy pilgrimage sites.
- Unveiling the Eternal Nature of Navadvipa: Bhaktivinoda Thakur vividly describes the eternal and transcendental nature of Navadvipa-dhama. It is not merely a geographical location but a spiritual abode that exists eternally, where Lord Chaitanya Mahaprabhu enacted His divine pastimes.
- Highlighting the Nine Islands (Nava-dvipa) and Their Significance: The Mahatmya meticulously details the

significance of the nine islands that constitute Navadvipa. Each island is associated with a specific aspect of devotional service and the pastimes of Lord Chaitanya and His associates, offering unique spiritual benefits to pilgrims.

- Emphasizing the Mercy and Love of Sri Chaitanya Mahaprabhu: A central theme is the unparalleled mercy and boundless love of Sri Chaitanya Mahaprabhu, which is especially potent and readily available in Navadvipa. The Mahatmya inspires devotees to take shelter of Mahaprabhu and experience this divine grace.

- Encouraging Pilgrimage and Devotional Practices in Navadvipa: The Sri Navadvipa-dhamaMahatmya serves as a powerful invitation and guide for devotees to undertake pilgrimage to Navadvipa. It describes the spiritual benefits of residing in or visiting this holy land and engaging in various devotional practices there, such as kirtana, hearing Krishna-katha, and serving the devotees.

7) Navadvipa sataka

Author: Prabodhananda Sarasvati

- One Hundred Verses on Navadvipa: A collection of one hundred poetic verses glorifying the holy land of Navadvipa, the birthplace of Sri Chaitanya Mahaprabhu.
- Description of Navadvipa's Spiritual Significance: Highlights the unique transcendental qualities and importance of this sacred place.

- Connection to Sri Chaitanya's Pastimes: Emphasizes the association of Navadvipa with the life and activities of Sri Chaitanya and his associates.
- Evocation of Devotional Atmosphere: Creates a vivid and inspiring picture of the spiritual ambiance of Navadvipa.
- Inspiring Pilgrimage and Devotion: Aims to cultivate deep reverence for Navadvipa and inspire devotees to visit and connect with its spiritual essence.

8) Sri Sri Navadvipa Bhava Taranga

Author: Bhaktivinoda Ṭhākura

1. **Meditation on Navadvipa Dham:** This book is a devotional poem or song cycle primarily focused on guiding the reader through an internal meditation (*bhajana*) on the holy land of Navadvipa, the birthplace of Sri Chaitanya Mahaprabhu.
2. **Essence of Navadvipa Lila:** Bhaktivinoda Thakura describes the various places within Navadvipa and connects them to the pastimes (*lilas*) of Chaitanya Mahaprabhu and His associates, revealing the spiritual significance of each location.
3. **Cultivation of Devotional Mood:** The text aims to help practitioners develop a deep spiritual attachment (*bhava*) to Navadvipa Dham, fostering an inner vision of the Lord's eternal presence and activities there.
4. **Revealing Mayapur as Goloka's Counterpart:** It elucidates the theological concept that Navadvipa

(specifically Mayapur) is non-different from Vrindavana and Goloka (Krishna's eternal abode), being the place where the most confidential *lilas* of Gauranga (Chaitanya Mahaprabhu) are eternally manifest.

5. **Aids for Internal Worship:** "Navadvipa Bhava Taranga" serves as a crucial text for those engaged in *raganuga-bhakti*, providing the framework for internal remembrance and service within the spiritual landscape of Navadvipa.

9) Jagannatha Mandir

Author: Bhaktivinoda Ṭhākura

1. **Glorification of Lord Jagannatha and His Temple:** This book is dedicated to describing the glories of Lord Jagannatha, His temple in Puri (Odisha), and the profound spiritual significance of this most sacred pilgrimage site.
2. **Historical and Traditional Insights:** Bhaktivinoda Thakura provides historical context and traditional accounts related to the Jagannatha temple, including its construction, the unique form of the Deities, and the long-standing devotional practices associated with them.
3. **Understanding Jagannatha's Lila and Mercy:** The text delves into the specific pastimes of Lord Jagannatha, emphasizing His immense mercy and the unique way He accepts the service of His devotees, especially through the Ratha-yatra (chariot festival).

4. **Puri Dham as a Sacred Space:** It highlights the spiritual potency of Puri Dham itself, describing its various holy places and their connection to Lord Jagannatha and Sri Chaitanya Mahaprabhu, who resided there for many years.

5. **Inspiring Pilgrimage and Devotion:** "Jagannatha Mandir" serves to inspire deep devotion to Lord Jagannatha and encourages Vaishnavas to understand the spiritual depth of the Puri pilgrimage, fostering a desire to participate in His worship and festivals.

<u>PASTIMES DIVINE</u>

"Since all Kṛṣṇa's pastimes are taking place continuously, at every moment some pastime is existing in Consequently these pastimes are called eternal by the Vedas and Purāṇas."

-Srila Prabhupada CC Madhya 20.395

The pastimes (lila) of Krishna are central to Gaudiya Vaishnava devotion. These divine activities, described primarily in the Srimad-Bhagavatam, are not considered mundane historical events but eternal, transcendental displays of the Lord's love, beauty, and power. Of particular significance are Krishna's childhood pastimes in Vrindavan, including His playful interactions with the cowherd boys and girls, His stealing of butter, lifting of Govardhan Hill, and His intimate, loving exchanges with the gopis, especially Radha. The rasa-lila, the divine dance of Krishna with the gopis, is considered the pinnacle of divine love. Understanding and meditating upon these pastimes, under the guidance of a bona fide spiritual master, is a crucial practice for cultivating bhakti, as it allows the devotee to enter into the personal realm of the Lord.

1) Gopala Campu

Author: Jiva Goswami

- A poetic masterpiece describing Krishna's eternal pastimes in Vrindavan.
- Presents the lila in two parts: Purva (early pastimes) and Uttara (later pastimes including leaving Vrindavan and

reunion).

- Richly details the relationships, moods, and settings of Vrindavan.
- Intended to nourish devotional meditation on Krishna's lila.
- Blends high philosophical concepts within intricate narrative and poetic structure.

2) Vidagdha Madhava (Play about Krishna in Vrindavan)

Author: Rupa Goswami

- Detailed Exposition of Radha and Krishna's Early Love: VidagdhaMadhava meticulously portrays the blossoming romance between Radha and Krishna during their youth in Vrindavan. It vividly describes their initial meetings, mutual attraction, and the development of their deep affection.
- Elaborate Descriptions of Vrindavan's Beauty: The play features rich and poetic descriptions of the transcendental abode of Vrindavan. It highlights the natural beauty of the forests, rivers, and hills, setting a captivating backdrop for the divine love story.
- Introduction of Key Supporting Characters: The VidagdhaMadhava introduces and develops important sakhis (female friends) of Radha and sakhas (male friends) of Krishna. These characters play crucial roles in facilitating the divine couple's meetings and enhancing the emotional depth of the narrative.

- Emphasis on Divine Playfulness and Wit: The title itself, VidagdhaMadhava ("The Clever or Expert Krishna"), suggests the prominence of playful interactions and witty exchanges between Radha and Krishna and their associates. The dialogues are often filled with cleverness, humor, and double meanings, reflecting the joyous nature of their pastimes.
- Foundation for Understanding Higher Aspects of Radha-Krishna Relationship: While focusing on the early stages of their relationship, VidagdhaMadhava lays the groundwork for understanding the more profound and complex aspects of Radha-Krishna prema (love) that are further elaborated in RupaGoswami's other works, such as Ujjvala-nilamani. It establishes the foundational principles of their eternal loving exchanges.

3) Lalita Madhava (Play about Krishna in Dwarka& reunion)

Author: Rupa Goswami

- The Pinnacle of Radha-Krishna's Union: Lalita-Madhava depicts the mature and most intimate stages of Radha and Krishna's divine love. It portrays their ecstatic union (milan) and the intense emotions associated with their relationship at its zenith.
- Central Role of Lalita-sakhi: The play prominently features Lalita-devi, one of Radha's closest and most important sakhis. She acts as a key orchestrator and

confidante in Radha and Krishna's pastimes, skillfully arranging their meetings and navigating the complexities of their love.

- Exploration of Intense Separation and Reunion: Lalita-Madhava delves deeply into the pangs of separation (viraha) experienced by Radha and Krishna, highlighting the profound emotional intensity of their love. The subsequent reunions are portrayed as moments of overwhelming joy and spiritual ecstasy.
- Elaborate Descriptions of Transcendental Emotions: The play provides intricate and poetic descriptions of the various bhavas (spiritual emotions) experienced by Radha, Krishna, and their associates. It explores the nuances of love, longing, jealousy (mana), and other ecstatic states in great detail.
- Theological Significance of Radha's Supreme Position: Lalita-Madhava subtly underscores the supreme position of SrimatiRadharani in the Gaudiya Vaishnava understanding of the divine couple. Her unique qualities and the depth of her love for Krishna are central to the narrative, illustrating her importance in the spiritual realm.

4) Dana Keli Kaumudi (Play about the "tax pastimes")

Author: Rupa Goswami

- The Divine Tax-Collecting Pastime: The central theme of Dana-keli-kaumudi revolves around the enchanting pastime of Radha and Krishna engaging in playful tax collection (dana-keli) on the path in Vrindavan. Krishna, disguised as a tax collector, playfully stops the gopis (cowherd girls), demanding payment for crossing "his" territory with their milk, yogurt, and butter.

- Highlighting the Sweetness and Intimacy of Radha-Krishna's Interactions: The play beautifully portrays the sweet and intimate exchanges between Radha and Krishna and their respective associates during these playful encounters. The dialogues are filled with wit, humor, and subtle expressions of their deep love and affection.

- Showcasing the Devotion and Loyalty of the Gopis: Dana-keli-kaumudi vividly illustrates the intense devotion and unwavering loyalty of the gopis towards Radha and Krishna. Their willingness to engage in these playful arguments and their clever retorts highlight their deep connection and love for the divine couple.

- The Art of Divine Flirtation and Teasing: The drama expertly captures the art of divine flirtation and teasing (narma) that characterizes the relationship between Radha and Krishna. These playful interactions serve to deepen their bond and provide immense spiritual bliss to the devotees who contemplate them.

- Revealing the Joyful and Lighthearted Aspects of the Spiritual Realm: Unlike narratives that focus solely on intense separation or profound philosophical discussions, Dana-keli-kaumudi offers a glimpse into the joyful and lighthearted aspects of the spiritual realm of Vrindavan. It underscores the playful intimacy and loving camaraderie that permeate the divine pastimes.

5) Ananda Vrindavana Campu (Poetic work on Vrindavan)

Author: Kavi Karnapura

- A Lush and Vivid Poetic Depiction of Vrindavan: The Campu offers an extraordinarily rich and imaginative poetic portrayal of the transcendental land of Vrindavan. Through elaborate descriptions and evocative language, KaviKarnapura brings to life the beauty, serenity, and spiritual atmosphere of Krishna's sacred abode.
- Focus on the Daily Pastimes of Radha and Krishna: The work intricately weaves together the daily pastimes (lila) of Radha and Krishna within the forests, groves, and along the banks of the Yamuna in Vrindavan. It captures the intimate details of their interactions with the gopis and gopas, highlighting the sweetness and joy of their eternal activities.
- Integration of Diverse Poetic Styles and Meters: Ananda-Vrindavana-Campu is renowned for its masterful use of various Sanskrit poetic styles and meters. KaviKarnapura's literary skill shines through in the lyrical flow and rhythmic beauty of the verses, creating a captivating reading experience.
- Emphasis on the Blissful and Joyful Nature of Vrindavan: The title itself, "The Blissful Forest of Vrindavan," underscores the central theme of joy (ananda). The Campu emphasizes the inherent bliss and spiritual ecstasy that permeate Vrindavan and the pastimes enacted there. It aims to immerse the reader in

this atmosphere of divine happiness.

- A Significant Contribution to Gaudiya Vaishnava Literature: As a prominent work by a direct disciple of Sri Chaitanya Mahaprabhu, Ananda-Vrindavana-Campu holds significant importance in Gaudiya Vaishnava literature. It provides a deeply devotional and poetically sophisticated understanding of Vrindavan and the eternal love between Radha and Krishna, influencing subsequent generations of devotees and scholars.

6) Sri Krishna Vijaya

Author: Gunaraja Khan

- Early Bengali Epic: An important early work in Bengali literature narrating the life and pastimes of Lord Krishna.
- Cultural and Linguistic Significance: Provides insights into the cultural and linguistic landscape of Bengal during its composition.
- Popularization of Krishna's Stories: Played a role in disseminating the stories of Krishna to a wider Bengali audience.
- Devotional Narrative: Presents the Krishna lila (pastimes) with a strong devotional sentiment.
- Influence on Later Bengali Vaishnavism: Likely influenced subsequent Bengali Vaishnava literature and devotional practices.

7) Sangeeta madhava

Author: VishvanathaChakravarti Thakur

- A Drama with Songs about Krishna: A theatrical work that narrates the pastimes of Lord Krishna through dialogue and devotional songs.
- Combination of Literature, Drama, and Music: Integrates different art forms to create a multi-sensory devotional experience.
- Focus on Krishna's Sweetest Pastimes: Likely depicts the most intimate and charming lilas of Radha and Krishna.
- Engaging and Accessible Presentation: Presents complex theological and devotional concepts in an engaging and emotionally resonant manner.
- Use in Devotional Performance: Intended for theatrical performance to inspire devotion and understanding among audiences.

8) Krsna Samhita

Author: Bhaktivinoda Ṭhākura

1. **Analytical & Philosophical Defense of Krishna's Supremacy:** "Krsna Samhita" is a profound philosophical treatise that analytically establishes Krishna as the Supreme Personality of Godhead, synthesizing Vedic evidence to refute impersonalistic

and polytheistic interpretations of divinity.

2. **Harmonization of Diverse Scriptural Views:** Bhaktivinoda Thakura masterfully reconciles seemingly contradictory statements from various Vedic scriptures regarding Krishna's position, demonstrating how all diverse spiritual paths ultimately culminate in the worship of Krishna.

3. **Refutation of Impersonalism and Material Misconceptions:** The book systematically refutes Mayavadi impersonalism and other philosophical deviations, providing clear arguments for the personal nature of God and the reality of His divine pastimes.

4. **Categorization of Krishna's Forms and Abodes:** It scientifically categorizes Krishna's different forms (e.g., Svayam Bhagavan, Svayam-prakasa, etc.) and His various abodes (Vrindavana, Goloka, Vaikuntha), explaining their distinct natures and glories.

5. **Primer for Educated Seekers:** Written in a scholarly yet accessible style, it was intended to appeal to educated individuals of Bhaktivinoda Thakura's time who were exposed to Western thought, providing a rational and systematic presentation of Gaudiya Vaishnava theology.

9) Camatkar Candrika

Author:Visvanatha Chakravarti Thakura

1. **Exposition of Ecstatic Vraja-lila Encounters:** "Camatkar Candrika" ("The Moonbeam of Astonishing Wonders") is a unique and intimate literary work that

vividly describes various astonishing and charming encounters between Krishna and the *gopis* in Vrindavana.

2. **Focus on Humorous and Playful Pastimes:** Unlike some other *lila* descriptions that focus on more intense emotions, this book often highlights the playful, humorous, and sometimes bewildering interactions that occur during Krishna's daily activities with the *gopis* and other Vraja residents.

3. **Revealing the Depth of Vraja-bhava (Mood of Vrindavana):** Through these seemingly simple or lighthearted pastimes, Visvanatha Chakravarti Thakura reveals the extraordinary depth of love, spontaneity, and unalloyed affection that characterizes the residents of Vrindavana.

4. **Poetic and Evocative Language:** The text is celebrated for its beautiful poetic language and evocative descriptions, which transport the reader into the enchanting atmosphere of Krishna's Vrindavana *lilas*.

5. **Aids Meditative Absorption:** It serves as a valuable resource for advanced practitioners of *raganuga-bhakti*, providing specific, delightful *lilas* for internal meditation (*bhavana*), helping them cultivate an intimate connection with the moods and activities of the Divine Couple and their associates.

10) Krsna lila stava

Author: Sanatana Goswami

1. **Comprehensive Hymn of Krishna's Pastimes:** "Krsna-lila-stava" is a majestic and extensive hymn (or prayer in verses) that glorifies the entire spectrum of Krishna's pastimes, from His appearance in Vrindavana to His later *lilas* in Mathura and Dvaraka, and even His return to Goloka.

2. **Narrative-Devotional Style:** It is structured as a series of verses that chronologically recount Krishna's *lilas*, simultaneously expressing deep devotion and offering elaborate prayers to the Lord for each pastime.

3. **Emphasis on the Sweetness of Lila:** Sanatana Goswami, one of the foremost disciples of Chaitanya Mahaprabhu, focuses on revealing the inherent sweetness (*madhurya*) and captivating nature of Krishna's activities, inspiring profound love in the reader.

4. **Authored by a Direct Disciple of Chaitanya:** As a direct associate of Chaitanya Mahaprabhu and a principal Goswami, Sanatana's description of Krishna's *lilas* carries immense authority and is deeply imbued with the *bhava* (spiritual emotion) that Chaitanya Mahaprabhu Himself taught and exemplified.

5. **Guide for Lila-Smaranam (Remembrance of Pastimes):** The systematic recounting of *lilas* makes it an excellent text for *lila-smaranam*, the practice of remembering and meditating on Krishna's divine pastimes, which is a key aspect of advanced devotional service.

11) Upakhyane Upadesa

Author: Bhaktivinoda Ṭhākura

1. **Moral and Spiritual Lessons Through Anecdotes:** "Upakhyane Upadesa" ("Instructions Through Stories/ Anecdotes") is a collection of short stories, parables, and anecdotes through which Srila Bhaktivinoda Thakura conveys profound moral, ethical, and spiritual teachings.
2. **Practical Application of Dharma and Bhakti:** The book aims to make complex philosophical concepts and principles of *dharma* (righteous conduct) and *bhakti* (devotional service) easily understandable and applicable to everyday life through relatable narratives.
3. **Simple Language for Broader Audience:** Written in a straightforward and accessible style, it was intended to educate and inspire a wide audience, including those who might not be able to delve into complex philosophical treatises.
4. **Addressing Common Misconceptions:** Many of the stories subtly or directly address common misconceptions, superstitions, and deviations prevalent in society and within religious practices, guiding the reader towards pure devotion.
5. **Instilling Vaishnava Values:** Each *upakhyana* (anecdote) concludes with a clear moral or spiritual lesson, helping to instill Vaishnava values such as humility, honesty, detachment, devotion, and surrender.

12) Krsna- the Supreme Personality of Godhead

Author: A.C. Bhaktivedanta Swami Prabhupada

1. **Narrative Retelling of Srimad-Bhagavatam's Tenth Canto:** This book is a direct, engaging, and comprehensive narrative retelling of the Tenth Canto of Srimad-Bhagavatam, which describes the pastimes of Lord Krishna.

2. **Focus on Krishna's Vrindavana Lila:** While it covers Krishna's entire manifest pastimes, it places a strong emphasis on His enchanting childhood and youth *lilas* in Vrindavana, highlighting their sweetness, intimacy, and transcendental nature.

3. **Accessible for a Global Audience:** Srila Prabhupada compiled this book specifically to present Krishna's pastimes to a Western and global audience, using clear, simple language and a captivating storytelling style.

4. **Philosophical and Devotional Significance Explained:** Though a narrative, Prabhupada includes crucial philosophical insights and devotional explanations, allowing readers to understand the spiritual significance of each pastime and develop love for Krishna.

5. **Gateway to Deeper Study:** Often serving as an entry point for newcomers to Krishna consciousness, it inspires readers to delve deeper into Srimad-Bhagavatam and other Vedic scriptures.

<u>PERSONAL ESOTERIC PERSPECTIVES</u>

"He delivered His most esoteric teachings on the subject of love of God to Rāmānanda Rāya, a member of a lower caste. Another of the Lord's disciples, Haridāsa Ṭhākura, was born a Muslim and was thus considered an outcast in Hindu society. Yet Śrī Caitanya elevated him to the exalted position of nāmācārya, the exemplar of the chanting of the holy name of Kṛṣṇa. Śrī Caitanya judged people not by their social status but by their spiritual advancement."

-Srila Prabhupada Chant and be happy ch 5

From an esoteric perspective, Gaudiya Vaishnavism offers a profound journey into the most intimate aspects of divine love. It goes beyond mere intellectual understanding of God, aiming for a direct, heartfelt realization of one's eternal relationship with Radha and Krishna. This involves cultivating a particular bhava (spiritual emotion or mood) in one's devotional service, often aiming for the mood of a gopi or a close associate of the divine couple in Vrindavan. This is known as raganuga-bhakti, spontaneous loving devotion, which transcends the regulative principles and aims for direct participation in the Lord's intimate pastimes. The esoteric understanding also delves into the concept of rasa – the transcendental mellows or tastes of divine love – enabling devotees to experience the various nuanced flavors of their relationship with God, culminating in madhurya-rasa, the conjugal mellow, considered the sweetest and most complete. This is a path of deep personal transformation, guided by advanced devotees and revelation, leading to an experience of divine intimacy that is unparalleled.

<u>Read these books very carefully and at mature stage of bhakti</u>

1) *Ujjvala nilamani (The Brilliant Sapphire of Conjugal Love)*

Author: Rupa Goswami

- An advanced sequel to Bhakti-rasamrita-sindhu, focusing exclusively on madhurya-rasa (conjugal love).
- Details the characteristics and categories of the hero (Krishna) and heroines (gopis, especially Radharani).
- Analyzes the various types of loving exchanges, moods, and ecstasies within madhurya-rasa.
- Describes the stimulants (uddipana) and expressions (anubhava) of conjugal love.

- Establishes the supremacy of Radharani and the unique position of the gopis' love.

Śrī Ujjvala-nīlamaṇi, also by RupaGoswami and likely completed in the mid-16th century, focuses on the detailed analysis of madhurya-rasa, the mellow of conjugal love for Krishna. Its core emphasis points are: the categorization of heroes (nayakas) and heroines (nayikas) in the context of madhurya-rasa; the description of the divine love between Radha and Krishna; the elaboration on the various stages and nuances of amorous devotional sentiments; and its recognition as the crest jewel of books describing the love for Krishna. This text delves into the most intimate and cherished aspect of Gaudiya Vaishnava theology – the loving relationship with Krishna in the mood of the gopis.

2) Śrī Vilāpa Kusumāñjali (An Offering of Flowers in Grief)

Author: Raghunatha dasa Goswami

- Profound Expression of Separation and Intense Longing for Radha-Krishna: The Vilāpa-kusumāñjali is a collection of heart-wrenching prayers and lamentations expressing RaghunathadasaGoswami's intense feelings of separation (viraha) from Radha and Krishna and his deep yearning to serve them in the spiritual realm of Vrindavan. It's a raw and deeply personal outpouring of devotional emotion.

- Focus on the Author's Unworthiness and Deep Humility: Throughout the verses, RaghunathadasaGoswami consistently portrays himself as utterly unqualified and filled with material attachments, repeatedly expressing his unworthiness to attain the service of the Divine Couple. This profound humility is a central characteristic of the work.
- A Vivid Portrayal of Vrindavan and the Divine Couple's Pastimes: Despite the mood of separation, the prayers are saturated with vivid descriptions of the transcendental beauty of Vrindavan and the enchanting pastimes (lila) of Radha and Krishna. This remembrance intensifies the devotee's longing to participate in those eternal activities.
- A Model of Advanced Raganuga Bhakti (Spontaneous Devotion): The Vilāpa-kusumāñjali is considered a quintessential example of raganuga bhakti, specifically in the mood of intense longing (utkantha). It showcases the depth of emotional absorption and the specific desires for service that characterize this advanced stage of devotional practice, driven purely by love and attraction.
- A Source of Inspiration and Guidance for Aspiring Devotees: While the intensity of the emotions expressed might seem overwhelming, the Vilāpa-kusumāñjali serves as a powerful source of inspiration and guidance for devotees striving to deepen their own connection with Radha and Krishna. It reveals the depth of love and yearning that is possible and encourages sincere and persistent devotion.

3) Govinda Lilamrita (The Nectar of Govinda's Pastimes)

Author: Krishna Dasa Kaviraja Goswami

- Describes the intricate daily pastimes (ashta-kaliya-lila) of Radha and Krishna in Vrindavan.
- Provides detailed visualizations for advanced devotional meditation (raga-marga).
- Focuses on the confidential loving exchanges within madhurya-rasa.
- Elaborates on the services performed by the gopis and manjaris.
- A guide for internal absorption in the divine lila.

4) Madhurya Kadambini (A Cloud Bank of Sweetness)

Author: Visvanath Chakravarti Thakur

- A short but profound work analyzing the stages of development in bhakti.
- Focuses on the role of divine grace (kripa) in the devotee's progress.
- Describes the subtle obstacles and tests faced on the path of devotion.
- Explains how bhakti progresses from initial faith (sraddha) to pure love (prema).

- Highlights the sweetness and allure of devotional service.

ŚrīMadhurya-kādambinī (A Cloud Bank Showering the Sweet Nectar of Sri Krishna) by ViśvanāthaCakravartīṬhākura instructs on the ways of bhakti yoga, focusing on: the stages of development in bhakti; the nature and cause of bhakti; the causeless mercy of Sri Krishna Chaitanya Mahaprabhu; the sweetness (madhurya) of Krishna; and the importance of a devotee's mercy in attaining bhakti. This book showers the sweet nectar of Sri Krishna and devotion to Him.

5) Raga Vartma Chandrika (Moonlight on the Path of Spontaneous Devotion)

Author: Visvanath Chakravarti Thakur

- Explains the distinction between regulated devotion (vaidhi-bhakti) and spontaneous devotion (raganuga-bhakti).
- Provides guidance for practitioners aspiring to follow the path of raganuga-bhakti.
- Details the process of cultivating internal service (manasi-seva) following the mood of Vrindavan residents.
- Warns against premature imitation (sahajiyaism) and emphasizes eligibility.
- Clarifies the relationship between external practice (sadhana) and internal meditation (smaranam).

6) Prakrita Rasa Shata Dushani (A Hundred Warnings Against Mundane Mellows)

Author: Bhakti siddhanta Sarasvati Thakur

- A forceful critique of imitating advanced devotional stages (rasa) prematurely (sahajiyaism).
- Warns against mistaking material emotions for spiritual ecstasy (prakrita-rasa vs. aprakrita-rasa).
- Emphasizes the necessity of purification through regulated practice (sadhana) before experiencing genuine rasa.
- Condemns deviations and cheapening of high devotional mellows, especially madhurya-rasa.
- Stresses adherence to authentic guru-parampara and scriptural injunctions.

7) Brihad Vaishnava Toshani (Commentary on Bhagavatam, Canto 10)

Author: Sanatana Goswami

- Detailed Explanation of Rasa-lila: A primary focus of the Toshani is to elaborate on the rasa-lila of Lord Balarama and his deep affection for the residents of Vraja. It delves into the intricacies of these divine pastimes, revealing profound aspects of love and devotion.

- Emphasis on Devotional Service (Bhakti): The commentary extensively discusses various aspects of bhakti, or devotional service to Lord Krishna. It sheds light on the principles and practices that cultivate a loving relationship with the Supreme Lord.
- Elucidation of Krishna's Names and Forms: Brihad Vaishnava Toshani provides insights into the numerous names and transcendental forms of Lord Krishna, deepening the understanding of His divine nature and glories.
- Clarification of Shridhara Swami's Commentary: SanatanaGoswami wrote this elaborate commentary to expand upon the points that Shridhara Swami had covered briefly in his own Bhavartha-dipika commentary on the Bhagavatam. The Toshani offers more detailed explanations, particularly from a devotional perspective.
- Conveying the Sweetness of Chaitanya Mahaprabhu's Teachings: The Brihad Vaishnava Toshani is imbued with the madhurya (sweetness) of the Gaudiya Vaishnava tradition as propagated by Sri Chaitanya Mahaprabhu. It aims to convey the profound love and ecstatic devotion that are central to this school of thought.

8) Krishna-Bhavanamrita

Author: Vishvanatha Chakravarti Thakur

- Nectar of Absorption in Krishna: Focuses on cultivating deep absorption and loving remembrance of Lord Krishna.
- Detailed Descriptions of Krishna's Qualities: Elaborates on the captivating beauty, charm, and transcendental attributes of Krishna.
- Emphasis on the Moods of Vrindavan: Explores the intimate and loving atmosphere of Krishna's pastimes in Vrindavan.
- Guidance on Internalized Devotion: Provides insights into developing a rich inner life of devotion and contemplation on Krishna.
- Evocative Language and Imagery: Uses poetic and evocative language to inspire deep feelings of love and attraction for Krishna.

9) Hamsaduta

Author: Rupa Goswami

- The Messenger Swan: A lyrical poem depicting a gopi (cowherd maiden) sending a swan as a messenger to Krishna.
- Exquisite Poetic Expression: Showcases RupaGoswami's mastery of Sanskrit poetry and literary artistry.
- Depiction of Intense Separation: Vividly portrays the deep pangs of separation felt by the gopis for Krishna.
- Elaboration on Krishna's: Describes the captivating qualities of Krishna that enchant the hearts of the gopis.

- Illustrates the Nature of Divine Love: Offers a glimpse into the intense and selfless love that the devotees have for Krishna.

10) Uddhava Sandesha

Author: Rupa Goswami

- Uddhava's Message: A poem narrating the message that Uddhava carries from Krishna in Dwarka back to the gopis in Vrindavan.
- Theology of Separation and Reunion: Explores the complex emotions of separation and the anticipation of reunion in the context of divine love.
- Philosophical Instructions: Contains profound philosophical instructions given by Krishna through Uddhava.
- Consolation for the Devotees: Offers solace and encouragement to those feeling separation from the Lord.
- Deep Insights into Krishna's Mind: Reveals Krishna's thoughts and feelings for His devotees in Vrindavan.

11) Bhavana-sara-sangraha

Author: Jiva Goswami

- Compilation of Essential Devotional Moods: A concise work that gathers and elucidates the most important bhavas (devotional moods or sentiments) experienced by devotees.
- Categorization of Devotional Attitudes: Systematically presents different types of loving relationships with Krishna, such as servitude (dasya), friendship (sakhya), parental affection (vatsalya), and conjugal love (madhurya).
- Guidance on Cultivating Specific Bhavas: Offers insights into how devotees can cultivate and deepen their particular chosen bhava in relation to Krishna.
- Emphasis on the Importance of Bhava in Bhakti: Underscores the crucial role of genuine devotional feeling in the practice of bhakti yoga.
- Practical Guide for Internalizing Devotion: Serves as a practical guide for devotees seeking to enrich their inner life of devotion and connect with Krishna on an emotional level.

12) Śrī Kṛṣṇa-Karṇāmṛta (Nectar for Krishna's Ears)

Author: Bilvamangala Thakura

- **Author:** It was composed by Bilvamangala Thakura (also known as Lilashuka), a renowned devotee-poet from South India, likely in the 13th century.

- **Essence of Krishna's Sweetness:** The title itself means "The Nectar for Krishna's Ears," signifying that the verses are so sweet and pleasing that they are fit to be heard by Krishna himself. The book is a profound meditation on the enchanting beauty and pastimes of Lord Krishna.

- **Focus on Krishna's Form and Lilas:** The work primarily focuses on the physical beauty, charming features, and various playful pastimes (*lilas*) of Lord Krishna, especially in his youthful form as a cowherd boy in Vrindavan. It's rich in vivid descriptions that evoke deep devotion.

- **Devotional Ecstasy (Bhakti-rasa):** It's celebrated for its intensely devotional mood, immersing the reader in *bhakti-rasa*, particularly *madhurya-rasa* (the sweetness of divine love). The verses often express the author's personal longing, adoration, and spiritual ecstasy.

- **Influence on Gaudiya Vaishnavism:** Śrī Kṛṣṇa-karṇāmṛta is highly revered and frequently quoted by subsequent Vaishnava acharyas, particularly within the Gaudiya Vaishnava tradition. Sri Chaitanya Mahaprabhu himself is said to have relished this work, further cementing its significance.

13) Śrī Gīta-govinda (Song about Govinda)

Author: Jayadeva Goswami

- **Author and Period:** Composed by the great Sanskrit poet Jayadeva, who lived in the 12th century CE, likely in Odisha, India.

- **Central Theme - Radha and Krishna's Love:** The work primarily narrates the divine and passionate love story of Radha and Krishna, focusing on their separation (vipralambha) and joyous reunion (sambhoga) in the groves of Vrindavan.

- **Literary Form - Kāvya and Opera:** It's a unique literary masterpiece that blends the poetic beauty of a *kāvya* (ornate Sanskrit poetry) with the dramatic structure of a mini-opera or lyrical drama, incorporating dialogues, emotions, and descriptions.

- **Musicality and Emotional Depth:** Each canto (chapter) is structured into *prabandhas* (songs) with specific *ragas* (melodic modes) and *talas* (rhythmic cycles), making it highly musical. It's renowned for its profound emotional depth, exploring various facets of *madhura-rasa* (conjugal love).

- **Profound Religious and Cultural Influence:** Beyond its literary merit, Gīta-govinda holds immense spiritual significance, particularly in the Bhakti traditions of Vaishnavism (especially Gaudiya Vaishnavism and Odia Vaishnavism). It's widely sung, recited, and interpreted as an allegory for the soul's longing for and ultimate union with the Divine.

14) Radha Rasa Sudha Nidhi

Author: Prabodhananda Sarasvati

- **Glorification of Sri Radha:** The central theme is the unparalleled glorification of Sri Radha, emphasizing her supreme position as the beloved consort of Lord Krishna and the source of all divine bliss.

- **Essence of Divine Love (Rasa):** The text delves deeply into the concept of *rasa*, the transcendental mellows of divine love, with Radha embodying the quintessence of *mahabhava* (the highest love for Krishna).

- **Intimate Pastimes (Lila):** It vividly describes the intimate and enchanting pastimes (*lila*) of Radha and Krishna in Vrindavan, often from the perspective of a *manjari* (a confidential maidservant of Radha).

- **Longing for Radha's Service:** A prominent sentiment expressed throughout the work is the author's intense longing and prayer to attain direct service to Sri Radha in Vrindavan, highlighting the path of *manjari-bhava*.

- **Radha's Compassion and Mercy:** The verses frequently extol Radha's immense compassion and mercy, describing how her glance or touch can bring ultimate spiritual fulfillment and relieve all suffering.

- **Krishna's Subservience to Radha's Love:** It portrays Lord Krishna as being completely captivated and even subservient to Radha's love, illustrating her power to enchant the enchanter himself.

- **Importance of Vrindavan:** Vrindavan is depicted as the sacred abode where these divine pastimes eternally unfold, and where one can experience the nectar of Radha's love.

- **Transcendence of Material Desires:** The book encourages devotees to renounce all material desires and worldly attachments, focusing solely on the pursuit of divine love for Radha and Krishna.

- **Poetic and Meditative Nature:** The work is highly poetic, filled with rich imagery and devotional fervor, making it a powerful tool for meditation on the divine couple.
- **Nectar of Devotion:** "Radha Rasa Sudha Nidhi" is considered a treasure trove of devotional nectar, guiding aspiring devotees towards a deeper understanding and experience of Radha-Krishna prema.

15) Prema Vivarta

Author: Jagadananda Pandita

- **Emphasis on the Supremacy of Prema (Divine Love):** The central theme of "Prema Vivarta" is the ultimate supremacy and transformative power of *prema*, pure divine love for Radha and Krishna. Jagadananda Pandita eloquently describes how *prema* is the highest goal of human life, surpassing even *mukti* (liberation).
- **The Glories of Lord Chaitanya Mahaprabhu:** The book extensively glorifies Lord Chaitanya Mahaprabhu as the most merciful incarnation of the Supreme Lord, who personally descended to distribute *prema* to the fallen souls of Kali-yuga through the *sankirtana* movement (congregational chanting of the Holy Names). It highlights Chaitanya Mahaprabhu's unique contribution of *unnatonatta-rasa*, the exalted loving sentiments of the residents of Vrindavan.

- **Renunciation and Avoidance of Offenses:** A significant portion of the book is dedicated to emphasizing the importance of genuine renunciation (*vairagya*) as a prerequisite for developing *prema*. Jagadananda Pandita strongly condemns hypocrisy, sense gratification disguised as devotion, and various offenses against Vaishnavas and the Holy Name, asserting that these are obstacles to the attainment of divine love.
- **The Stages of Devotional Development:** While not a systematic exposition like some other philosophical texts, "Prema Vivarta" touches upon the progressive stages of devotional service, from *sraddha* (faith) to *bhava* (spiritual ecstasy) and finally *prema*. It describes the internal transformation that takes place as one advances in *bhakti*.
- **Essence of Vrindavan Bhava:** The book beautifully conveys the mood and internal feelings (*bhava*) of the residents of Vrindavan, particularly the *gopis*, in their unalloyed love for Krishna. It encourages readers to aspire for such pure, spontaneous devotion (*raganuga-bhakti*) by following in the footsteps of the Vrindavan devotees.

16) Ujjvala_Nilamani_Kiranah

Author: Śrīla Viśvanātha Cakravartī Ṭhākura

- **A Concise and Accessible Essence of Madhurya-Rasa:** While Srila Rupa Goswami's original "Ujjvala Nilamani" is a voluminous and intricate work, Visvanatha Chakravarti Thakura's "Kiranah" ("ray" or "essence") serves as a highly condensed and simplified presentation of its core teachings. He takes the *very essence* of Rupa Goswami's profound analysis of *madhurya-rasa* and renders it in a more digestible and easily understandable Sanskrit. It's often compared to "putting the entire ocean in a pot." This makes the advanced subject matter more accessible to serious students who might find the original daunting.

- **Visvanatha's Unrivaled Insight into the Dynamics of Divine Love:** Visvanatha Chakravarti Thakura was known as "Cakravarti," meaning "emperor of the *chakra* (cycle) of commentaries," a testament to his profound understanding of Vaishnava philosophy. In "Ujjvala Nilamani Kiranah," he applies his extraordinary spiritual realization and analytical prowess to illuminate the subtle interactions between Krishna (*nayaka*) and His beloveds (*nayikas*). He unpacks the various *bhava* (emotions) and their components with a precision that enriches the reader's appreciation of the divine loving exchanges. His explanations help clarify the psychological and emotional nuances of *madhurya-rasa*.

- **Reinforcement and Elucidation of Rupa Goswami's Classifications:** Visvanatha Thakura doesn't just summarize; he often provides further elucidation and justification for Rupa Goswami's classifications of heroes, heroines, their assistants, and the various conditions of love. For instance, when Rupa Goswami outlines the different types of *nayikas* (e.g., *mugdha, madhya, pragalbha*), Visvanatha's commentary might offer specific examples or deeper explanations to fully grasp their characteristics and how they interact with

Krishna. He helps the reader distinguish between subtle shades of emotions and relationships within *madhurya-rasa*.

- **Emphasis on the Transcendental Nature of *Parakiya-bhava* through Commentary:** The concept of *parakiya-bhava* (paramour love) in Vrindavan is a cornerstone of Gaudiya Vaishnava theology. Visvanatha Chakravarti Thakura, in his commentaries (including *Ananda-chandrika* on Ujjvala Nilamani and *Sarartha Darsini* on Srimad-Bhagavatam), not only accepts but strongly defends and elaborates on this concept as the highest and most intense form of love for Krishna. His "Kiranah" would certainly highlight this, emphasizing how the apparent "unorthodoxy" from a mundane perspective is actually the essence of pure, unconditional, and unbridled divine love in the spiritual realm, free from any material constraints or rules. He clarifies why it is superior to *svakiya-bhava* (married love) in the context of Vrindavan.

- **Practical Guidance for Meditative *Bhavana* and Internal Cultivation:** While scholarly, Visvanatha Chakravarti Thakura's writings are always infused with practical devotional application. His "Kiranah," by simplifying the complex subject, assists practitioners in their *bhajana* (spiritual practice) and *bhavana* (meditation). By clearly outlining the different types of *bhava* and *lila* dynamics, he provides the essential framework for advanced devotees to absorb themselves in the intimate pastimes of Radha and Krishna, cultivating a deeper internal connection and aspiring for *raganuga-bhakti*. He makes the esoteric more accessible for internal realization.

17) Sri Radhika-dhyanamrta

Author: Srila Visvanatha Chakravarti Thakura.

- **Focused on Srimati Radharani's Glories:** The book is entirely dedicated to glorifying Srimati Radharani. It systematically describes her transcendental beauty, auspicious bodily marks, ornaments, garments, and the various qualities that make her so dear to Lord Krishna and the supreme object of worship for Gaudiya Vaishnavas.
- **A Meditative Text (Dhyanamrta):** "Dhyanamrta" literally means "nectar of meditation." The verses are structured to facilitate deep, internal meditation (*dhyana*) on Radharani's form and attributes. Each verse often presents a specific aspect or characteristic of Radharani for the devotee to fix their mind upon, helping to develop a vivid internal visualization.
- **Emphasis on Her Prema-bhava (Loving Mood):** Beyond her physical beauty, the text subtly reveals Radharani's unparalleled *prema-bhava* (mood of divine love) for Krishna. It hints at the depth of her emotions, her service attitude, and her unique position as the embodiment of Krishna's complete loving potency (*hladini-sakti*).
- **Guidance for Raganuga-bhaktas:** For practitioners of *raganuga-bhakti* (spontaneous devotional service), who aspire to follow in the footsteps of the residents of Vrindavan, "Sri Radhika-dhyanamrta" is an invaluable

tool. By meditating on Radharani's form and *bhava* as described, devotees seek to cultivate a similar loving relationship with the Divine Couple.

- **Composition by a Rasika Acharya:** The author, Srila Visvanatha Chakravarti Thakura, is renowned as a "rasika acharya," one who has deep realized knowledge of transcendental *rasas* (mellows). His composition of "Sri Radhika-dhyanamrta" is a testament to his profound insight into the intimate loving pastimes of Radha and Krishna, offering a glimpse into the internal world of pure devotion.

CONCLUSION

In Gaudiya Vaishnavism, the spiritual journey from initial faith (Adho Shraddha) to pure love of God (Prema) is deeply facilitated by reading books from Gaudiya Acharyas. These texts, starting with foundational works like the Bhagavad-gita for solidifying initial belief, evolve into deeper scriptures like the Srimad Bhagavatam and Chaitanya Charitamrita that support Sadhu-sanga (association with devotees) and Bhajana-kriya (devotional practice). As a devotee progresses through stages like Anartha-nivrtti (cessation of unwanted habits), Niṣṭhā (steadiness), Ruci (taste), and Āsakti (attachment), These books provide the philosophical understanding and devotional mood, with works like Narottama Dasa Thakura's Prarthana and Prema Bhakti Chandrika, and Bhaktivinoda Thakura's Sharanagati, offering heartfelt prayers and practical guidance, ultimately illuminating the path to the profound realization of Bhāva and Prema.

<u>**In concluding this humble endeavor**</u> to present a summary of 108 foundational texts of Gaudiya Vaishnavism, it is with a sense of both fulfillment and the recognition of the vastness that still lies beyond. The ocean of wisdom contained within this tradition is truly boundless, with countless other illuminating scriptures, commentaries, and devotional works awaiting exploration. Should the Lord's grace and inspiration continue to flow, it is our deepest aspiration to delve further into this treasury and perhaps, in time, offer a subsequent volume to touch upon even more of these invaluable resources.

Finally, as the author of this humble attempt, I would be immensely grateful for **your valuable feedback. Your insights, observations, and suggestions will be invaluable in guiding any future endeavors.** Please feel free to share your thoughts on what resonated with you, what could be improved, and what aspects of this rich tradition you would be interested in exploring further. Your engagement is deeply appreciated in this shared journey of understanding and devotion.

For further information and important shlokas of books mentioned in this compendium, visit Harigopinath Das website https://harigopinathdas.com/ where I am sharing details of these shastras regularly.Please give your valuable feedback and correction on mail-dr.hari.gopinath.das@gmail.com

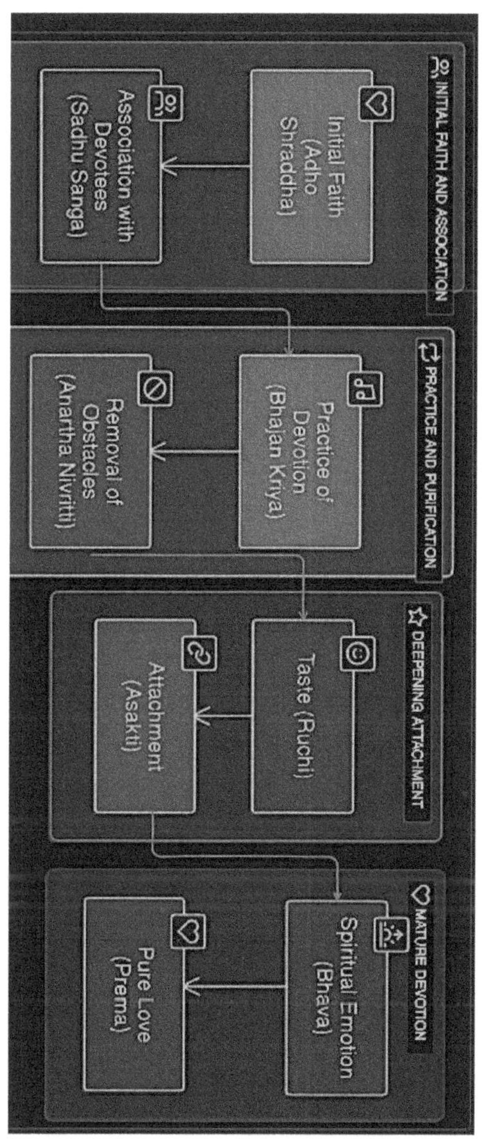

Flow of Bhakti -Role of Guru/Sadhu/Shastra(Books)

CHAPTER EIGHT

BONUS BOOKS 108+

The nectar flow continues !!

Gaudiya Math Books

- **Srila Bhakti Prajnan Kesava Goswami Maharaj (Founder of Sri Gaudiya Vedanta Samiti)**

Author of: Acintya-bhedābheda-siddhānta, Śrī Prema-bhakti-candrikā (commentary), numerous articles and lectures compiled into books.

A prolific writer and preacher, he upheld the pure philosophical conclusions of the Gaudiya Vaishnava tradition and published many significant texts, including his own works and commentaries on classical scriptures.

- **Srila Bhakti Rakshak Sridhar Dev-Goswami Maharaj (Founder of Sri Chaitanya Saraswat Math)**

Author of: Śrīmad Bhagavad-gītā: The Hidden Treasure of the Sweet Absolute, Śrī Caitanya-līlā-smaraṇa-maṅgalam, Śrī Śrī Prema-dhāma-deva Stotram, Śrī Guru-Darśan,

Loving Search for the Lost Servant.

Known for his profound philosophical insight, poetic language, and ability to present intricate Vaishnava conclusions in a deeply realized and accessible manner. His works are highly esteemed for their depth and devotional fervor.

- **Srila Bhakti Promode Puri Goswami Maharaj (Founder of Sri Gopinath Gaudiya Math)**

Author of: Art of Sadhana, Sri Chaitanya Mahaprabhu: His Life and Precepts, numerous articles and short books.

A long-standing and respected figure, he was the chief editor of the Nadiya Prakash daily spiritual newspaper during and after Srila Bhaktisiddhanta's time. His writings focus on practical devotional life and the glory of Mahaprabhu's teachings.

- **Srila Bhakti Dayita Madhava Goswami Maharaj (Founder of Sri Chaitanya Gaudiya Math)**

Author of: Numerous Bengali books and articles, many of which are compilations of his lectures and instructions, often translated as Gaudiya Darshan.

He extensively preached throughout India, establishing many temples and branches. His works preserve and disseminate the teachings of the Gaudiya Math.

- **Srila Bhaktivedanta Narayana Goswami Maharaj (A prominent figure from the Sri Gaudiya Vedanta Samiti lineage)**

Author of: Extensive commentaries on many Goswami literatures (e.g., Śrīmad Bhakti-rasāmṛta-sindhu, Śrī Vilāpa-kusumāñjali, Śrī Harināma Cintāmaṇi, Śrī Gīta Govinda), as well as original works like Śrī Gauḍīya Darśana and numerous transcribed lectures.

Highly prolific in terms of translations and commentaries, he emphasized the confidential raganuga-bhakti (spontaneous devotional service) principles and made many classical Gaudiya texts accessible to a modern audience.

Disciples of Srila Prabhupada-

They recorded and preserved hundreds of audio and video lectures of Srila Prabhupada AND ALSO CONTINUED LEGACY OF WRITING

Srila Prabhupada-lilamrta by Satsvarupa dasa Goswami (Vol. 1: 1980 , Vol. 2: 1982 , Vol. 3: 1983, Vol. 4: 1980 , Vol. 5: 1981, Vol. 6: 1982, Vol. 7: 1983) is an extensive biography of Srila Prabhupada, chronicling his life and the early years of ISKCON.

- Detailed Biography: Śrīla Prabhupāda-līlāmṛta is a comprehensive biographical account of the life of A.C. Bhaktivedanta Swami Prabhupada, the founder of the International Society for Krishna Consciousness (ISKCON).
- Authoritative Source: The book is considered a primary and authoritative source for understanding Srila Prabhupada's life, teachings, and contributions.
- Chronological Narrative: It provides a chronological narrative of Srila Prabhupada's life, starting from his

birth and childhood, through his spiritual journey, and his efforts in establishing ISKCON and spreading Krishna consciousness globally.

- Personal Insights: The book includes personal stories, conversations, and observations from Srila Prabhupada's disciples and associates, offering intimate glimpses into his personality, interactions, and mission.
- Spiritual Legacy: Śrīla Prabhupāda-līlāmṛta emphasizes Srila Prabhupada's profound spiritual legacy, highlighting his role as a spiritual leader, translator, and commentator of Vedic scriptures, and his impact on millions of people worldwide.

Watering the Seed by Giriraj Swami (2010) shares personal realizations and experiences in the association of Srila Prabhupada.

- Srila Prabhupada's Care:
- The book showcases Prabhupada's tireless efforts to nurture the spiritual growth of his disciples, particularly Giriraj Swami, like watering a seed.
- Personal Realizations:
- Giriraj Swami shares his own spiritual experiences, demonstrating how his association with Prabhupada led to deeper understanding and realization.
- Fatherly Love:
- The book highlights Prabhupada's gentle and compassionate nature towards his disciples, emphasizing his role as a spiritual father.
- Unwavering Determination:
- Prabhupada's unwavering commitment to spreading Krishna consciousness, even in the face of challenges, is

a key theme.
- Philosophical Insights:
- The book offers glimpses into Prabhupada's philosophical perspectives, both in times of crisis and in everyday life.

A Living Theology of Krishna Bhakti: Essential Teachings of A. C. Bhaktivedanta Swami Prabhupada by Tamal Krishna Goswami (2012) explores the theological contributions of Srila Prabhupada.

- Prabhupada's Synthesis: The book demonstrates how Prabhupada integrated Vedic knowledge, particularly the Bhagavad Gita and Srimad-Bhagavatam, with the principles of Gaudiya Vaishnavism, a devotional tradition centered on Krishna.
  The "Living Theology": Goswami argues that Prabhupada's teachings are not merely a static philosophy but a dynamic, living theology that guides individuals on their path of spiritual self-realization.
  Emphasis on Bhakti: The book highlights Prabhupada's profound emphasis on bhakti, the cultivation of loving devotion towards Krishna, as the primary means of spiritual progress.
  Krishna as the Supreme Personality of Godhead: Prabhupada's teachings, as explored in the book, firmly establish Krishna as the ultimate object of worship and the source of all spiritual power.
  Practical Applications: The book provides insights into the practical aspects of Prabhupada's teachings, including the importance of chanting the Hare Krishna mantra, engaging in devotional service, and cultivating a loving relationship with Krishna.

The Lives of the Vaishnava Saints: Shrinivas Acharya, Narottam Das Thakur, and Shyamananda Pandit by Steven J. Rosen (2002)

- The book aims to provide insights into the lives and teachings of these prominent Vaishnava saints, offering a deeper understanding of their contributions to the tradition and their lasting impact. It also explores the context of their lives within the broader history of the Vaishnava movement.
- Shrinivas Acharya: Known for his role in establishing the Goswami lineage and spreading the teachings of Chaitanya Mahaprabhu.
- Narottam Das Thakur: Famous for his devotional poetry and songs, which are still cherished by Vaishnavas today.
- Shyamananda Pandit: Recognized for his leadership and contributions to the Vaishnava movement, particularly in spreading devotion.

Gaudiya Vaisnava Biographies and Samadhis in Vrndavana by Mahanidhi Swami (2013)

- Spiritual Perfection: The book reveals teachings on spiritual perfection from the lives of the saints.
- Hidden Truths: It delves into the hidden meanings behind the samadhis of these devotees.
- Practical Guidance: It provides instructions on how to approach the samadhis, offer prayers, and connect with the saints.
- Direct Experience: The book encourages readers to seek a direct connection with the saints through these sacred sites.

- Essence and Practice: It helps devotees understand the essence of Gaudiya Vaisnavism and how to practice its principles, particularly in relation to the samadhis of past saints.

The Heart of a Vaishnava: Exploring the Essence of Humility, Tolerance & Compassion in the Life of God's Servants by B. P. Puri

- 1. Humility: Vaishnavas recognize the Supreme Lord as the ultimate authority and acknowledge their own insignificance in comparison. This humility leads to a sense of service and devotion to God and others.

  2. Tolerance: Vaishnavas are taught to respect all religions and to see the divine presence in all beings, regardless of their background or beliefs. This tolerance promotes unity and understanding.

  3. Compassion: The book highlights the Vaishnava ideal of caring for all beings, particularly those in need. This compassion is expressed through acts of service, charity, and empathy.

  4. Devotion: Vaishnava faith emphasizes the importance of devotion to the Supreme Lord. This devotion is expressed through prayer, chanting, and service.

  5. Living a Life of Principle: The book encourages followers to live their lives according to the principles of Vaishnavism, striving to be humble, tolerant, and compassionate in all their actions and interactions.

- **I'll Build You a Temple: The Juhu Story** by Giriraj Swami (2021) narrates the challenges and triumphs in establishing the Hare Krishna temple in Juhu, Bombay.

- **Many Moons: Reflections on Departed Vaishnavas** by Giriraj Swami (2012) offers appreciations of senior devotees of Srila Prabhupada.
- **Vaisnava Behavior: The Twenty-Six Qualities of a Devotee** by Satsvarupa dasa Goswami (2004) describes the characteristics and conduct of a devotee of Krishna.
- **Miracle on Second Avenue: Hare Krishna Arrives in the West** by Mukunda Goswami (2011) chronicles the early days of the Hare Krishna movement in the West.
- **Ocean of Mercy: A Search Fulfilled** by Bhakti Charu Swami (2016) is a memoir recounting the author's experiences with Srila Prabhupada.
- **Chasing Rhinos With The Swami** by Shyamasundar Das (Vol. 1: 2016 , Vol. 2: 2017, Vol. 3: 2018) recounts the author's experiences as an early disciple of Srila Prabhupada.
- **Surrender Unto Me: An Overview of the Bhagavad-Gita** by Bhurijana Dasa (1997) provides an overview of the Bhagavad-Gita based on Gaudiya Vaishnava commentaries.
- **My Glorious Master: Remembrances of Prabhupada's Mercy on a Fallen Soul** by Bhurijana Dasa (1996) shares the author's memories of Srila Prabhupada.

Biographies of Gaudiya Vaishnava Personalities

- **Prabhupada: Messenger Of The Supreme Lord** by Satsvarupa dasa Goswami (Biography of Srila Prabhupada)
- **The Six Goswamis of Vrindavan** by Steven J. Rosen
- **Conversations with the Saint** by author Gopal Krishna Goswami

- **Mayapur-Vrindavan Festivals With Srila Prabhupada (1972-77)** by Loknath Swami Maharaj
- **Yamuna Devi: A Life of Unalloyed Devotion**
- **Srila Bhaktivinoda Thakura** by Bhakti Pradip Tirtha
- **Prabhupad Saraswati Thakur**
- **Three Apostles of Gaudiya Vaishnava Movement** by Tridandi Sri Bhakti Prajnan Yati Maharaj (1994)
- **The Nectarean Glories of Sri Nityananda** by Bhakti Sundar Govinda
- **The Heart of a Vaishnava: Exploring the Essence of Humility, Tolerance & Compassion in the Life of God's Servants** by B. P. Puri
- **Srila Prabhupada in Calcutta**
- **Padayatra Worldwide- On the road with Lord Caitanya**
- **HH Bhakti Damodar Maharaj** (also known as Dr. Damodar Prasad Dasa prior to sannyasa) is a respected scholar and sannyasi within ISKCON, known for his work in reconciling modern science with Vedic wisdom. His contributions primarily focus on bridging the perceived gap between scientific understanding and the principles of Krishna consciousness. His books, though often technical in nature, aim to demonstrate that the Vedic paradigm, particularly as presented in the Śrīmad-Bhāgavatam and by Srila Prabhupada, offers a more complete and coherent explanation of reality than materialistic science alone. Through his writings, he critiques the limitations of reductionist science while presenting Vedic cosmology, consciousness, and metaphysics as a superior framework for understanding the universe and life itself, thus reinforcing the scientific validity of spiritual principles.

- Cosmic Theogony
- Vedic Paradigm of Consciousness
- The Paradox of Darwinism
- The Universe as a Living Entity
- Vedic Cosmology and Physics: A Paradigm Shift (or similar titles in this vein)

Books by HH Radhanath Swami Maharaj

105 The Journey Home:Autobiography of an American Swami (2008): This is Radhanath Swami's acclaimed memoir, recounting his incredible journey as Richard Slavin, a young American seeker who traveled overland from Chicago to India in the 1970s. It details his encounters with various spiritual teachers, his years of searching, and his eventual acceptance of the path of Gaudiya Vaishnavism. The book offers insights into mystic traditions and the challenges of self-discovery.

106 The Journey Within: Exploring the Path of Bhakti (2016): This book serves as a practical guide to the principles of Bhakti Yoga, the yoga of love and devotion. Drawing from ancient wisdom and contemporary life, Radhanath Swami explores essential questions about love, the soul, and God, offering readers tools and insights to deepen their spiritual connection in everyday life.

- **Evolve: 2 Minute Wisdom (2014):** This book presents concise, two-minute readings designed to inspire reflection and positive change. It offers practical wisdom applicable to daily challenges and encourages readers to cultivate inner peace and purpose through short, impactful messages.

- **The Real You:** The Practice of Self-Discovery (2014): This book delves into the concept of self beyond the physical body and mind, guiding readers on a journey of self-discovery rooted in spiritual understanding. It explores themes of identity, purpose, and the potential for inner fulfillment through spiritual practices.
- **Soul-wise (2010/2011):** This book offers insights into the nature of the soul and its journey. It explores themes of inner peace, resilience, and finding deeper meaning in life by connecting with one's spiritual essence.
- **The Wisdom Tree:** Bringing Wisdom Into Lives (2012/2013): This book presents teachings aimed at bringing spiritual wisdom into practical aspects of life. It covers various topics relevant to personal growth, relationships, and finding balance through a spiritual lens.
- **Nectar Stream (2014):** This book likely contains further reflections and insights from Radhanath Swami, continuing the themes of spiritual growth, devotion, and practical application of ancient wisdom in modern life.

107 Conversations with the Saint by HH Gopal Krishna Goswami

- Dialogues and teachings: The book is a collection of conversations and teachings.
- A spiritual luminary: The source of these dialogues and teachings is a spiritual teacher.
- Gopal Krishna Goswami's spiritual experiences: The author's own spiritual experiences inform his writing.

Books By HH Bhanu Swami Maharaj

His Holiness Bhanu Swami Maharaj is renowned for his extensive translation work of significant Gaudiya Vaishnava texts from Sanskrit and Bengali into English. He has translated over fifteen major works, with more in progress. Some of the key translations include:

1. **Sad Sandarbhas of Srila Jiva Goswami:** This monumental philosophical work comprising six parts (*Tattva-sandarbha*, *Bhagavat-sandarbha*, *Paramatma-sandarbha*, *Krishna-sandarbha*, *Bhakti-sandarbha*, and *Priti-sandarbha*).

2. **Sarartha-darshini commentary on Srimad Bhagavatam by Srila Vishvanatha Chakravarti Thakura:** This is a comprehensive translation of the renowned commentary on the Srimad Bhagavatam.

3. **Gita-bhusana commentary on Bhagavad-gita by Srila Baladeva Vidyabhushana.**

4. **Commentaries on the Srimad Bhagavatam by Srila Jiva Goswami (Vaisnava Tosani).**

5. **Commentaries on the Brahma-samhita by Srila Jiva Goswami.**

6. **Commentary on Sri Isopanisad by Srila Baladeva Vidyabhushana.**

7. **Bhakti-rasamrta-sindhu with commentaries by Srila Jiva Goswami and Srila Vishvanatha Chakravarti Thakura.**

8. **Ujjvala-nilamani with commentaries by Srila Jiva Goswami and Srila Vishvanatha Chakravarti Thakura.**

9. **Laghu-bhagavatamrta with Baladeva Vidyabhushana's commentary.**

10. **Krishna-karnamrta with Krishnadasa Kaviraja Goswami's commentary.**

11. **Gopala-campu by Srila Jiva Goswami.**

12. **Hari-bhakti-vilasa with Dig-darshani commentary by Srila Sanatana Goswami.**
13. **Caitanya-siksamrita by Srila Bhaktivinoda Thakura.**
14. **Ananda-vrndavana-campu by Sri Kavikarnapura.**
15. **Sri Madhava-mahotsava of Sri Jiva Goswami.**
16. **Bhavartha-sangraha of Sri Kavikarnapura.**
17. **Krsnaahnika-kaumudi of Sri Kavikarnapura.**
18. **Madhurya Kadambini commentary by Srila Visvanatha Chakravarti Thakura.**
19. **Dana-keli-kaumudi.**
20. **Hamsaduta and Uddhava Sandesa.**
21. **Ascarya-Rasa-Prabandhah.**
22. **Sri Chamatkara Candrika.**
23. **Sri Govinda Lilamrta.**

Books Authored/Compiled by Bhanu Swami Maharaj: While his primary contribution has been through translations, Bhanu Swami Maharaj has also authored and compiled books based on his lectures and studies:

1. **Attainment of Suddha Nama & Suddha Bhakti (Volumes 1 & 2):** Compilations of his Srimad Bhagavatam classes and seminars.
2. **Sarartha Darshini:** This title appears to be used for his English translation of Srila Vishvanatha Chakravarti Thakura's commentary on Srimad Bhagavatam, but it might also refer to compilations of his own insights on the text.
3. **Principal Upanisads:** Translations and explanations of various Upanishads like *Aitareya, Kena, Svetasvatara, Mandukya, Prasna, and Taittiriya Upanisad.*
4. **Kali-Santarana Upanishad - Caitanya Upanishad Explanation of Mahamantra.**

5. **Krsna Janma Tithi Vidhi.**

6. **Prema - Vivarta by Jagadananda Pandita** (Translation and possibly commentary).

7. **Sri-Radha-Rasa-Sudha-Nidhih** (Translation and possibly commentary).

8. **Sri Caitanya Candramrta** (Translation and possibly commentary).

9. **Siddhanta Ratnam - Gem of Conclusions.**

10. **Sri Sankalpa Kalpadruma - The Desire Tree of Vows.**

11. **Narada-Bhakti-Sutra & Sandilya-Bhakti-Sutra & Jitante Stotram** (Translation and possibly commentary).

12. **Vaisnavanandini Commentary on Srimad Bhagavatam** (various cantos and volumes).

13. **Rasika Ranjana and Vidvad Ranjana by Srila Bhaktivinoda Thakura** (Translation).

14. **Govinda Dasera Kadaca** (Translation).

15. **Gayatri Vyakhya (Explanation of Gayatri Mantra from Agni Purana).**

16. **Sri Radha-Krsnarcana-Dipika** (Translation and possibly commentary).

17. **Radha-Krsna Ganoddesa-Dipika** (Translation).

18. **Sri Caitanya Siksamrta - The Nectarean Instructions of Lord Caitanya** (Translation).

19. **3 Books of Srila Bhaktivinoda Thakura's** (Compilation and Translation).

20. **Bhakti Tattva Vivek** (Translation and possibly commentary).

21. **Sri Madhava Mahotsava** (Translation).

22. **Dasa Mula Tattva** (Translation and possibly commentary).

23. **Nikunja-Keli-Virudavali** (Translation and possibly commentary).

24. Sri Vrndavana Mahimamrta (Translation).
25. Preyo-Bhakti-Rasarnava (Translation).
26. Bhaktayaloka.
27. Krshnahnika Kaumudi (Translation).
28. Sri Vraja Riti Cintamani (Translation and possibly commentary).
29. Yogasara Stava Tika (Translation).
30. Sri-Vilapa-Kusumanjalih (Translation).
31. Sri Krsna Bhavanamrta (Translation).
32. Sri Aisvarya Kadambini (Translation and possibly commentary).
33. Sangita Madhava (Translation).
34. Datta Kaustubha (Translation).
35. Amnaya-Sutra (Translation).
36. Tattva-Sutras (Translation).
37. Tattva-Viveka (Translation).
38. Defining Parakiya & Defeating Svakiya (Translation).
39. Prema Pradipa (Translation).
40. Siddhanta Ratnam (Translation).
41. Vedanta Syamantaka (Translation).
42. Harinama Cintamani (Translation).
43. Bhajana-Rahasya (Translation).
44. Nama Kaumudi

<u>And many more books </u>by the disciple and <u>Grand disciples of Srila Prabhupada</u> which are connecting counless people to Krishna Holy Name -
Hare Krishna Hare Krishna Krishna Krishna Hare Hare
Hare Ram Hare Ram Ram Ram Hare Hare !!

CHAPTER NINE

Gaudiya Vaishnava terminologies

1. **Acintya-bhedabheda:** The philosophy of inconceivable oneness and difference between Krishna and His energies (including the jivas and the material world).
2. **Adhikari:** One who is qualified to understand or practice a particular aspect of spiritual life.
3. **Anartha:** Unwanted habits or material attachments that hinder spiritual progress.
4. **Antaranga Shakti:** The internal potency of the Lord, also known as *svarupa-shakti*, which manifests His personal abode and associates.
5. **Archa-vigraha:** The deity form of the Lord, worshipped in temples and homes.
6. **Bahiranga Shakti:** The external potency of the Lord, which manifests the material world.
7. **Bhagavan:** The personal aspect of the Absolute Truth, possessing all six opulences in full: strength, fame, wealth, knowledge, beauty, and renunciation.
8. **Bhajan:** Devotional singing and chanting.
9. **Bhakti:** Pure devotional service to the Lord, the ultimate means of liberation and attaining love of God.

10. **Brahman:** The impersonal aspect of the Absolute Truth.
11. **Dharma:** One's eternal occupational duty, which for the jiva is to serve Krishna.
12. **Guru:** The spiritual teacher who guides the disciple on the path of bhakti.
13. **Ishvara:** The Supreme Controller, the Supreme Personality of Godhead, Krishna.
14. **Jiva:** The individual living entity, an eternal part and parcel of Krishna.
15. **Jnana:** Knowledge, especially knowledge of the self and the Supreme.
16. **Karma:** Action and its reactions, which bind the jiva to the cycle of birth and death.
17. **Kirtan:** Congregational chanting of the holy names of the Lord.
18. **Maya:** Illusion, the energy of the Lord that covers the jivas' true nature and binds them to the material world.
19. **Moksha:** Liberation from the cycle of birth and death.
20. **Paramatma:** The Supersoul, the localized aspect of Krishna residing in the hearts of all living beings and atoms.
21. **Prakriti:** Material nature, composed of three modes: sattva (goodness), rajas (passion), and tamas (ignorance).
22. **Prasadam:** Food offered to the Lord with devotion and then distributed as His mercy.
23. **Prema:** Pure love of God, the highest goal of life in Gaudiya Vaishnavism.
24. **Purusha:** The enjoyer; refers primarily to Krishna as the supreme enjoyer and secondarily to the jivas identifying with prakriti.
25. **Rasas:** The different mellows or flavors of devotional love experienced in relation to Krishna.

26. **Sadhu:** A holy person, a devotee dedicated to spiritual life.
27. **Samsara:** The cycle of birth, death, old age, and disease in the material world.
28. **Sankirtan:** The congregational chanting movement popularized by Sri Chaitanya Mahaprabhu.
29. **Seva:** Selfless service rendered to Krishna and His devotees.
30. **Shakti:** The potencies of the Lord.
31. **Shastra:** Revealed scriptures, such as the Bhagavad-gita and Srimad-Bhagavatam, considered the ultimate authority.
32. **Tatastha Shakti:** The marginal potency of the Lord, consisting of the jivas.
33. **Tattva:** Philosophical truth or principle.
34. **Vairagya:** Detachment from material possessions and sense gratification.
35. **Yoga:** Linking oneself with the Supreme; in Gaudiya Vaishnavism, primarily refers to bhakti-yoga.
36. **Avatara:** Incarnation of the Lord who descends to the material world for a specific purpose.
37. **Lila:** The divine pastimes of the Lord.
38. **Dham:** The holy abode of the Lord, such as Vrindavan and Navadvipa.
39. **Murti:** Another term for the deity form of the Lord.
40. **Siddhanta:** Established philosophical conclusion.
41. **Sad-guru:** A genuine and qualified spiritual teacher.
42. **Chaitanya Mahaprabhu:** The incarnation of Krishna who appeared in Navadvipa, Bengal, in the 15th century and propagated the chanting of the holy names.
43. **Rupa Goswami and Sanatana Goswami:** Two of the six Goswamis of Vrindavan, principal disciples of Chaitanya Mahaprabhu and important theologians of Gaudiya

Vaishnavism.

44. **Radha:** The eternal consort and most beloved devotee of Krishna, representing the epitome of *mahabhava* (the highest form of love).

45. **Gopis:** The cowherd girls of Vrindavan, Krishna's most intimate associates who exemplify selfless love.

46. **Madhurya-rasa:** The mellow of conjugal love for Krishna, considered the highest of the five primary rasas in Gaudiya Vaishnavism.

47. **Dasya-rasa:** The mellow of servitude to Krishna.

48. **Sakhya-rasa:** The mellow of friendship with Krishna.

49. **Vatsalya-rasa:** The mellow of parental affection for Krishna.

50. **Shanta-rasa:** The mellow of neutrality or peaceful reverence towards Krishna.

CHAPTER TEN

Gaudiya Vaishnava Personalities

In Gaudiya Vaishnava philosophy, **Sri Krishna** is not merely a historical figure or an incarnation, but Svayam Bhagavan, the Supreme Personality of Godhead Himself, the original source of all incarnations and expansions. He eternally resides in His spiritual abode of Goloka Vrindavana, displaying the most intimate and enchanting pastimes (lilas). His advent on Earth approximately 5,000 years ago in Mathura, and His subsequent upbringing in Vrindavana by Nanda Maharaja and Mother Yasoda, was a display of His internal potencies, meant to attract all souls to His loving service. His lilas are characterized by unparalleled sweetness, beauty, and charm – from His childhood pranks to His heroic feats and, most importantly, His amorous pastimes with the gopis.

Srimati Radharani is Krishna's eternal consort and the expansion of His internal pleasure potency (hladini-sakti). She is the supreme devotee and the embodiment of maha-bhava, the highest expression of divine love. Her beauty, qualities, and love for Krishna are unmatched, and she is considered the Queen of Vrindavana and the source of all the gopis. All the gopis are expansions of her loving mood and serve as her faithful companions and assistants in facilitating Krishna's pleasure. Radha and Krishna are one, eternally united in a transcendental loving exchange, and their lilas are the zenith of spiritual relationships.

Their associates in Vrindavana are not ordinary beings but eternally liberated souls who participate in Krishna's divine lilas according to their specific loving relationships (rasas). These include:

Nanda Maharaja and Mother Yasoda: Krishna's foster parents, representing vatsalya-rasa (parental affection), whose unalloyed love is characterized by deep care and protection.

The Cowherd Boys (e.g., Subala, Sridama): Krishna's intimate friends, representing sakhya-rasa (fraternal friendship), who enjoy playful sports and adventures with Him, treating Him as their equal.

The Gopis (e.g., Lalita, Visakha, Citra, Campakalata, Tungavidya, Indulekha, Rangadevi, Sudevi - the Asta-sakhis): The confidential female associates of Radharani, representing madhurya-rasa (conjugal love). They are the zenith of devotion, eternally serving Radha and Krishna in their most intimate pastimes, under the leadership of Srimati Radharani. Their love is pure, spontaneous, and entirely dedicated to the pleasure of the Divine Couple.

The Cows, Calves, and Natural Elements of Vrindavana: Even the seemingly inanimate aspects of Vrindavana are considered conscious participants in Krishna's lilas, contributing to the beauty and joy of His eternal abode.

Pioneers of the Gaudiya Tradition

The Pancha-Tattva

They are the five principal manifestations of the Supreme Absolute Truth who descended together as companions of Sri Chaitanya Mahaprabhu to propagate the yuga-dharma of hari-nama-sankirtana (congregational chanting of the Holy Names) in the Kali-yuga. They are:

- **Sri Chaitanya Mahaprabhu:** The Supreme Personality of Godhead (Krishna Himself), appearing as His own devotee to teach love of Godhead.
- **Nityananda Prabhu:** The immediate expansion of Sri Chaitanya Mahaprabhu (Balarama), manifesting as the embodiment of divine mercy and compassion.
- **Advaita Acharya:** A combined incarnation of Maha-Vishnu and Sadasiva, who prayed intensely for Lord Chaitanya's descent.
- **Gadadhara Pandita:** An incarnation of Srimati Radharani's spiritual potency (hladini-sakti), embodying the internal devotional mood.
- **Srivasa Thakura:** An incarnation of Narada Muni, representing the pure devotee and the head of all devotees.

Svarupa Damodara Goswami (c. 1490-c. 1560): Intimate associate of Chaitanya, recorded his teachings and pastimes, and a key figure in the early theological development.

Seven Goswamis

Rupa Goswami (1489-1564): One of the Six Goswamis of Vrindavan, principal architect of Gaudiya Vaishnava theology, wrote foundational texts like Bhakti-rasamrita-sindhu and Upadeshamrita.

Sanatana Goswami (1488-1558): Another of the Six Goswamis, contributed significantly to the philosophical and ethical framework with works like Brihad-bhagavatamrita and Hari-bhakti-vilasa.

Jiva Goswami (c. 1513-c. 1598): The foremost philosopher among the Six Goswamis, systematized Gaudiya Vaishnava theology in works like Sat-sandarbhas.

Gopala Bhatta Goswami (c. 1503-c. 1578): One of the Six Goswamis, established important standards for deity worship.

Raghunatha Dasa Goswami (1495-1586): One of the Six Goswamis, known for his intense renunciation and devotion, author of Stavavali.

Raghunatha Bhatta Goswami (c. 1505-c. 1579): One of the Six Goswamis, expert in reciting Srimad-Bhagavatam.

Murari Gupta (c. 1475-c. 1555): Early associate of Chaitanya, his chronicle is one of the earliest biographies.

Vasudeva Datta Thakura (dates unknown): Known for his immense compassion and desire to take on the suffering of others.

Shivananda Sena : A key figure who facilitated the annual journey of devotees to Puri.

Later Acharyas and Key Figures:

Krishnadasa Kaviraja Goswami (c. 1496-c. 1588): Author of the monumental biography of Chaitanya Mahaprabhu,

Chaitanya Charitamrita.

Narottama Dasa Thakura (c. 1540-c. 1611): A prominent acharya who popularized Gaudiya Vaishnava bhajans (devotional songs).

Shyamananda Prabhu (c. 1534-c. 1630): Another important acharya who spread the teachings in Orissa.

Srinivasa Acharya (c. 1535-c. 1620): A key figure in re-establishing the Gaudiya Vaishnava tradition in Bengal after the disappearance of the Six Goswamis.

Vishvanatha Chakravarti Thakura (c. 1638-c. 1734): A prolific commentator on the major Gaudiya Vaishnava texts, providing crucial insights.

Baladeva Vidyabhushana (c. 1700-c. 1768): A prominent scholar who defended Gaudiya Vaishnavism and wrote important commentaries, including Govinda-bhashya on the Vedanta-sutra.

Jagannatha Dasa Babaji (c. 1776-1894): A highly revered saint known for his advanced devotional state.

Bhaktivinoda Thakura (1838-1914): A pivotal figure in the modern revival of Gaudiya Vaishnavism, wrote extensively, and rediscovered important holy sites.

Gaurakisora Dasa Babaji (c. 1838-1915): A renunciate saint and the spiritual master of Bhaktisiddhanta Sarasvati Thakura.

Bhaktisiddhanta Sarasvati Thakura (1874-1937): The son of Bhaktivinoda Thakura, a dynamic preacher who established the Gaudiya Matha and sent disciples to the West.

A.C. Bhaktivedanta Swami Prabhupada (1896-1977): Founder of the International Society for Krishna Consciousness (ISKCON), translated and commented on major scriptures, and widely propagated Gaudiya Vaishnavism globally.

Other Significant Acharyas and Devotees:

Locan Dasa Thakura (c. 1520-c. 1580): Author of Chaitanya Mangala.

Vrindavana Dasa Thakura (c. 1507-c. 1589): Author of an early biography of Chaitanya Mahaprabhu, Chaitanya Bhagavata.

Kavi Karnapura (Parashuram Das) (c. 1524-c. 1600): Son of Shivananda Sena, wrote important biographical and philosophical works.

Prabodhananda Sarasvati : A renunciate scholar and author of devotional poetry.

Haridasa Thakura (c. 1450-c. 1510): A prominent early Muslim convert and a model of chanting the holy name.

Sarvabhauma Bhattacharya (c. 1458-c. 1547): A renowned scholar who was converted by Chaitanya Mahaprabhu and became a great devotee.

Ramananda Raya (c. 1475-c. 1540): A highly advanced devotee with whom Chaitanya Mahaprabhu had profound spiritual dialogues.

Madhavendra Puri (c. 1350-c. 1420): Considered a seminal figure whose teachings influenced Chaitanya Mahaprabhu.

Ishvara Puri : The spiritual master of Chaitanya Mahaprabhu.

Dhyanachandra Goswami : A prominent disciple of Rupa Goswami.

Narahari Chakravarti Thakura : Author of Bhakti-ratnakara.

Tirtha Maharaja (Kunjabihari Vidyabhushana) (1898-1960): A prominent disciple of Bhaktisiddhanta Sarasvati Thakura, a leading figure in the Gaudiya Matha.

Sridhara Maharaja (Bhaktiraksha Sridhara Deva Goswami) (1895-1988): A highly respected disciple of

Bhaktisiddhanta Sarasvati, founded Sri Chaitanya Saraswat Math, known for his profound philosophical insights and gentle demeanor.

Madhava Maharaja (Parivrajaka Acharya Kesava Goswami Maharaja) (c. 1889-1960): A leading disciple of Bhaktisiddhanta Sarasvati, known for his scholarship and preaching.

Vamana Maharaja (Acharya Tridandi Swami Srimad Bhaktiprajnana Vamana Goswami Maharaja) (1904-1989): A prominent disciple of Bhaktisiddhanta Sarasvati and a respected acharya.

Narayana Maharaja (Tridandi Swami Srimad Bhaktivedanta Narayana Goswami Maharaja) (1921-2010): A prominent disciple of A.C. Bhaktivedanta Swami Prabhupada and a significant teacher emphasizing the rasa aspect of Gaudiya Vaishnavism.

Bhakti Ballabha Tirtha Goswami Maharaja (1924-2017): A disciple of Bhaktisiddhanta Sarasvati Thakura and the president of Sree Chaitanya Gaudiya Math.

Bhakti Vaibhava Puri Maharaja (1943-2020): A disciple of Bhaktisiddhanta Sarasvati Thakura, a respected senior Vaishnava leader.

Modern Key Figures in ISKCON

Satsvarupa dasa Goswami (Stephen Guarino) (b. 1939): One of the first disciples, prolific author, artist, and senior leader in ISKCON.

Indradyumna Swami (b. 1949): A disciple of A.C. Bhaktivedanta Swami Prabhupada, known for his extensive preaching tours and the annual Festival of India.

Jayadvaita Swami (b. 1949): A senior disciple of A.C. Bhaktivedanta Swami Prabhupada, known for his meticulous editing and scholarship, particularly of Prabhupada's books.

Bhakti Charu Swami (1945-2020): A disciple of A.C. Bhaktivedanta Swami Prabhupada, known for his eloquent preaching and establishment of ISKCON Ujjain.

Gopal Krishna Goswami (b. 1944-2024): A senior disciple of A.C. Bhaktivedanta Swami Prabhupada, a member of the Governing Body Commission (GBC) of ISKCON, and a leader in India.

Giriraja Swami (1947): A senior disciple of A.C. Bhaktivedanta Swami Prabhupada, known for his leadership in developing ISKCON in Mumbai and his thoughtful guidance.

Sivarama Swami (b. 1949): A disciple of A.C. Bhaktivedanta Swami Prabhupada, a respected leader in Hungary and author of several books.

Radhanath Swami (b. 1950): A senior disciple of A.C. Bhaktivedanta Swami Prabhupada, a spiritual leader and author known for his community building and interfaith work.

Urmila Devi Dasi (Dr. Edith Best) (b. 1955): A disciple of A.C. Bhaktivedanta Swami Prabhupada, known for her work in education and women's issues within ISKCON.

Hanumatpresaka Swami (Dr. Edwin Bryant) (b. 1957): A disciple of A.C. Bhaktivedanta Swami Prabhupada, a renowned scholar of Sanskrit and Hindu scriptures, particularly the Srimad-Bhagavatam.

Hare Krishna !!

As you reach the end of this brief journey through the vast landscape of Gaudiya Vaishnava literature, I sincerely hope it has ignited a spark of curiosity and a deeper appreciation for the profound wisdom held within these sacred texts. This summary has offered but a glimpse, a preliminary introduction to the ocean of nectar left for us by our compassionate acharyas.

These 108 books are not mere historical artifacts; they are living rivers of divine knowledge, flowing directly from the hearts of realized souls. Within their pages lie the answers to life's most profound questions, the practical guidance for cultivating genuine love for the Supreme Lord, and the keys to unlocking our own inherent spiritual potential. They meticulously unravel the intricacies of the self, the nature of reality, the glories of the Divine Couple, Radha and Krishna, and the sublime path of bhakti-yoga.

While this book has aimed to provide a helpful overview, it is crucial to understand that it is merely an invitation – an encouragement to delve into the original sources. Imagine the difference between hearing about a delicious feast and actually tasting its exquisite flavors. Similarly, while a summary can inform, the direct experience of reading the words of Srila Rupa Goswami, Srila Sanatana Goswami, Srila Jiva Goswami, and countless other luminaries is transformative. Their insights, born of deep realization and unwavering devotion, carry a power that resonates directly with the soul.

Therefore, I urge you, dear reader, to make a sincere endeavor to engage with these original texts. Allow their wisdom to seep into your heart and illuminate your understanding. Let the profound philosophical discussions clarify your doubts, and let the devotional outpourings awaken the dormant love within you.

By dedicating even a small portion of your time to studying these books, you will undoubtedly:

Gain a deeper and more nuanced understanding of Gaudiya Vaishnava philosophy.

Strengthen your faith and conviction in the path of bhakti.

Receive direct guidance and inspiration for your spiritual practice.

Connect with the unbroken lineage of wisdom that stretches back to Lord Chaitanya Mahaprabhu.

Experience the profound joy and fulfillment that comes from genuine spiritual understanding.

The treasure is there, waiting to be discovered. Do not let the constraints of time deter you from accessing this invaluable inheritance. Even a few verses read and contemplated daily can bring about a profound shift in perspective and enrich your life immeasurably.

May this humble introduction serve as a catalyst, propelling you towards the inexhaustible wellspring of wisdom offered by our beloved acharyas. May their words illuminate your path and guide you towards the ultimate goal of love and devotion to Sri Radha and Krishna.

For further information and important shlokas of books mentioned in this compendium, visit Harigopinath Das website https://harigopinathdas.com/

List Of Books I Have Read !

Begin your journey......